What people are saying about…

# OVERCOMING
## *Mediocrity*©

5 out of 5 Stars
Powerful and Inspiring!

"*I enjoyed the openness and vulnerability of the author's stories. It gave me an emotional boost to learn how they all pushed through obstacles and came out stronger on the other side. It's true — we are all limitless. Learning to get out of our own way is essential to experiencing a limitless life.*"

—Therese

5 out of 5 Stars
Strong Women Share Powerful Advice!

"*This book has great advice and resources for women who want to accelerate their personal growth journey. There is something for everyone and I love that each writer is down to earth and easy to relate to.*"

—Melinda

5 out of 5 Stars
An Empowering Book!

"*An empowering book of strong woman discussing their life stories and successes! Their path to success and where they are today was not an easy path. I highly recommend reading this book. You will come away with some sage advice that may help you move the needle in your own life.*"

—M Good

5 out of 5 Stars
Incredibly Inspiring!

> "This book will make the reader jump off the couch and dive directly into their hopes and dreams. Told from a variety of viewpoints, these women show that anything is possible if one is willing to work hard for their dreams. The reader will be infused with hope and inspiration. I highly recommend reading this book and the rest of the Overcoming Mediocrity series of books from Christie Ruffino."

—Christine

5 out of 5 Stars
Extraordinary

> "Mediocrity. It's like having a fire in your life that's only smoldering. These women's stories are inspiring, irresistible, and motivating."

—Jack's Mum

5 out of 5 Stars
Couldn't Stop Reading... Loved It!

> "Pure gold! I would recommend this for anyone who is looking for stories of real people who have overcome challenges. Loved the specific strategies they shared and resources they provided."

—Little

5 out of 5 Stars
Excellent Read for Men and Women!

> "LOVED THE BOOK! [Husband] thought it should not be limited to a "women's" book — excellent for men and women. Writing was personal, intimate, yet clearly educational in nature. Long enough to take you somewhere, but short enough to sit down and read right then. The book is downloaded on our Kindle, so we can read again."

—TJ

5 out of 5 Stars
Inspirational on all New Levels!

*"What an amazing book. The power of these women is inspiring! Especially the story from 'Brittany' absolutely amazing, inspiring, and something anyone looking to summon inner strength should read!"*

—Robert

5 out of 5 Stars
Very Inspiring!

*"It is so great hearing how these women have not stopped in the face of life happening. In these times, this is needed more than ever. A great read for those who are looking to empower other women."*

—Lauren

5 out of 5 Stars
Wonderful Motivational Book! So Inspiring!

*Wonderful motivational book! Very uplifting stories. I bought a couple for my Christmas and birthday presents!"*

—Ericka

5 out of 5 Stars
Fearlessly and Wonderfully Made!

*"This book is so encouraging and uplifting I couldn't put it down. I originally got this book to support one of my dear friends but quickly fell in love with every story that I read. The encouragement that came from every story hit in every aspect of my life. I'm so grateful something like this was written. The younger generation definitely needs to hear stories and successful stories of women that suffer through some hard times and come out victorious!!"*

—Eden

5 out of 5 Stars
Very Inspiring!

*"Thank you, ladies, for telling your stories. So inspiring, love the book. Bought multiple copies to give to my girlfriends that are unstoppable woman in my life. Thank you."*

—Julie

5 out of 5 Stars
Highly Recommend!!

*"HIGHLY RECOMMEND!!! If you are looking for personal and professional development, this book is for you! It is perfectly inspiring, educational, empowering and beautifully written! I could really relate to the struggles in their personal stories and it has helped me to continue working on overcoming my own obstacles so I can succeed in life and in business! Thank you all for sharing your incredible journeys."*

—Lisa

5 out of 5 Stars
It's a Great Investment in Yourself!

*"This is an inspiring compilation. Each woman's story contains powerful lessons that are widely applicable. Heartwarming and triumphant all at the same time. Any woman who's tread a rocky path on her life's journey will be able to relate and rejoice along with each author as she overcomes adversity and challenge. If you're seeking inspiration to overcome adversity, take a moment to breathe, regroup, and soak up a story or three. It's a great investment in yourself."*

—Debbra

5 out of 5 Stars
Vulnerable and Real!

*"I appreciate the vulnerability of these women sharing their stories and sharing their healing strategies. A must read for inspiration."*

—A. Wade

What our clients are saying about...

# OVERCOMING *Mediocrity*©

*"I hit six figures in my first year, and I'm doing really well, thanks to Christie's coaching and the publicity that I was able to get from the overcoming mediocrity series. I can't recommend this experience highly enough. Joining the overcoming mediocrity team was a life-changing experience for me."*

—Lindsey Oaks
Personal Branding
*Overcoming Mediocrity Limitless Women*

*"Working with Christie and her team was just the nudge I needed to finally sit down and start writing. The social media tips that were provided when the book launched were invaluable for engaging and re-engaging people who follow me. I am much more confident about my next book, and its launch."*

—Valerie Mrak
Speaker • Filmmaker • Storyteller • Coach
*Overcoming Mediocrity Victorious Women*

*"Christie and her team made the process of becoming an Amazon Bestselling Author easy and fun. There are resources and support every step of the way, and now I have a book to grow my business."*

—Amanda Tobinski
Magnetic Media Group
*Overcoming Mediocrity Fearless Women*

"I cannot say enough about Christie Ruffino and her coaching! I found so much value that I chose to collaborate with her on the most recent publication of Overcoming Mediocrity. You will not be disappointed when you reach out to Christie for coaching in business, as the insight, tools, and coaching elements also translate to everyday life."

—Sara Goggin Young
Owner, Mindset, Nutrition, and Movement Coach
*Overcoming Mediocrity Limitless Women*

"Being an author in the latest book in the "Overcoming Mediocrity" series helped me break through a limiting block so I can share my story. Christie helped me gain confidence and realize that by sharing my story, I'm helping others and positioning myself as a subject matter expert. Now, I'm getting invited to be on other people's podcasts. I'm considering starting my own podcast as well. If you have an important story inside you, Christie and the company she founded has resources to help you share it in a big and impactful way."

—Therese R. Nicklas, CFP®, CMC®
Certified Financial Planner™ and True Wealth™ Coach
*Overcoming Mediocrity Limitless Women*

"Christie is a mission-driven woman who is changing the world by sharing the stories of amazing women. I was honored to be included in one of her bestselling books, and the benefits of that book keep unfolding in my life. The impact in my life started immediately with writing my story (an impactful internal journey to my own personal why), continued with the connections I made to the other women in the book AND in Christie's extensive network, and continues because I'm now a best-selling author, speaker, and podcaster. It really launched a whole new chapter in my life. If you are ready to embrace the next iteration of yourself and make a difference in the world, contact Christie."

—Maren Oslac
Heart & Sole Dance – Founder
*Overcoming Mediocrity Unstoppable Women*

*"If you're on the fence, I'd highly recommend and encourage you to jump in feet first because not only did I get to work with other amazing women, but I also ended up being an Amazon Bestselling Author which is a huge boost for my career and brand. I hope that you'll choose to share your inspiring story for all of the many women who are going to read it."*

—Amber Champagne-Matos
Founder of Champagne Apothecary
*Overcoming Mediocrity Unstoppable Women*

*"I'm passionate about helping women overcome the lies that are holding them back. The problem was that I still believed my own lies. I questioned if my story could actually make a difference, feared that no one would want to hear it and didn't trust I could write it well enough for it to be published. Until I met Christie. She invited me to share my story in one of her books, and it completely transformed my business, my life and best of all, the lives of the women who read it. They've reached out to me, grateful for how what I shared helped them overcome their adversities. Hearing those women's testimonies gave me confidence and fueled me to keep writing. With Christie's help, I published my own book just a few months later, and am currently writing the next in that series."*

—Shannon Ferraby
Author, Speaker & Trainer with Success Unwrapped
*Overcoming Mediocrity Influential Women*

*"When I learned about this project, I was already fully into the writing, publishing, and marketing process of my other book, Getting Yourself Unstuck. However, I couldn't put everything in that book. Therefore, Overcoming Mediocrity allowed me to publish a very personal story that didn't seem to fit in my other book. Now going forward in my marketing, the two books will work in tandem."*

—Angie Engstrom
Coach and Plank Trainer
*Overcoming Mediocrity Resilient Women*

"Being a part of this book made such a difference and I love the conversations that Christie and I had together. They were so rich and revealing that I actually can do a TED talk. But really, what really broke through for me is being able to share my story and to be a subject expert. Since then, I've been on other people's podcasts and I started my own podcast 'Tea Time Midlife Edition.' If you have a story that you want to share with the world, get in front of Christie."

—Regina Young
Podcaster and CEO of Modelperfect Woman
*Overcoming Mediocrity Unstoppable Women*

"Being an Amazon Bestselling Author alongside some fabulous women in this series has propelled me forward in ways that I wouldn't have had otherwise. I've since guested on podcasts, I have an episode on Amazon Fire TV, and I've had so many women tell me how inspired they've been by the book. Secondarily, I was able to tell my story in a really authentic way and not have it completely rearranged in the editing process. I'm really excited to see what the future holds."

—Tiffany Lewis
CEO of More Meaningful Marketing
*Overcoming Mediocrity Unstoppable Women*

"Christie Ruffino is a master at taking women's women who are passionate about telling their story, but they don't know exactly how they're going to do it and molding us into not only authors but Amazon Bestselling Authors. It was an amazing six-month journey, where I got to meet some amazing women, discover their stories, and realize that what I have to say is important and something that the world needs to hear."

—Danica Joan
Founder of Kids Need Both, Inc
*Overcoming Mediocrity Unstoppable Women*

"Me, an Amazon number one Bestselling Author. What a crazy exciting journey this has been and an accomplishment I would have never dreamed of. Joining the Overcoming Mediocrity project has brought me so many new connections, as well as the credibility and the credentials for my business. Becoming an author is something I never planned to do in my lifetime but has been a very, very exciting ride!"

—Laura Fank-Carrara
President of Laura Ocean Solutions
*Overcoming Mediocrity Unstoppable Women*

"Being an author in the series has opened doors for me. It makes it easier to rise to the top of the list for those responsible for booking speaking gigs to want to talk to me. The traffic to my website and Business Page has increased measurably. It has shortened the know, like, trust factor. People are reaching out to me first before I reach out to them. The titles of the books help women who want to stretch themselves. Who wouldn't want to associate themselves and work with an author who is Dynamic, Resilient, Strong, and Influential?"

—Jeanne Lyons
Career Breakthrough Coach
*Overcoming Mediocrity Influential Women*

"Christie and the OM team took an overwhelming and complicated process of book publishing and made it very easy to get my story published. I was guided through the process from start to finish. Every detail was outlined, and my questions were always answered promptly. The book has received rave reviews, and it has taken my credibility to the next level, as I am now an Amazon #1 best seller! Thank you!!"

—Lynn O'Dowd
Motivational Speaker and Keynote Performer
*Overcoming Mediocrity Influential Women*

# *Overcoming Mediocrity*

# Other Overcoming Mediocrity Titles

Overcoming Mediocrity — Dynamic Women

Overcoming Mediocrity — Courageous Women

Overcoming Mediocrity — Strong Women

Overcoming Mediocrity — Remarkable Women

Overcoming Mediocrity — Resilient Women

Overcoming Mediocrity — Influential Women

Overcoming Mediocrity — Victorious Women

Overcoming Mediocrity — Fearless Women

Overcoming Mediocrity — Unstoppable Women

Overcoming Mediocrity — Empowered Women

Overcoming Mediocrity — Limitless Women

# EPIC WOMEN
# OVERCOMING
## *Mediocrity*©

**A unique collection of stories from epic women
who have created their own lives of significance!**

Presented by Christie Lee Ruffino

## DPWN Publishing

www.OvercomingMediocrity.org

Copyright © 2023 by Dynamic Professional Women's Network, Inc.

All rights reserved. No portion of this book may be reproduced by mechanical, photographic, or electronic process, nor may it be stored in a retrieval system, transmitted in any form, or otherwise be copied for public use or private use without written permission of the copyright owner.

This book is a compilation of stories from numerous experts who have each contributed a chapter. It is designed to provide information and inspiration to our readers.

It is sold with the understanding that the publisher and the individual authors are not engaged in the rendering of psychological, legal, accounting, or other professional advice. The content and views in each chapter are the sole expression and opinion of its author and not necessarily the views of DPWN Publishing, Christie Lee Ruffino, or the Dynamic Professional Women's Network, Inc.

For more information, contact:
DPWN Publishing
A division of the Dynamic Professional Women's Network, Inc.
1879 N. Neltnor Blvd. #316, West Chicago, IL 60185
www.OvercomingMediocrity.org
www.OurDPWN.com

Printed in the United States of America

ISBN: 978-1-939794-30-7

# Dedication

To every woman who does not believe she can make a difference; and to every woman who believes she can move a mountain.

To every woman who continually makes sacrifices for those she loves; and to every woman who prioritizes those moments, when she can pamper and take care of her own needs.

To every woman who believes that she should settle for the life she has; and to every woman who has overcome great odds to create her own life of significance.

To the epic women in this book who've shared their stories with you; in hopes that their lessons of pain will become your lessons of power.

# The Power of a Story

There is nothing more important in this world than the relationships we build and the legacy we leave in the lives of those who've crossed paths with us on our journey of life. It's the experiences we have during this journey that define our individual uniqueness and create our own powerful personal blueprint or our unique story snowflake.

It is this blueprint that can empower and equip us to possess a distinct advantage over every other person in this world, if leveraged correctly and shared. If we don't have the courage to share our snowflake, it will be lost forever. No one will have the same story, and no one can repeat your story. Therefore, those who come after you will never learn anything from what you've experienced and what you've learned if you don't share it.

I feel that the most significant thing we can do to add value back to this world, is to master the narrative of our lives. All of our leadership and moneymaking abilities rest in our ability to discover, craft, and deliver our personal story or message in a way that will allow people to connect to us. The right story shared at the right time with the right person can alter the trajectory of their life, as well as our own.

I have also discovered, how therapeutic the process of owning our story is for us to become ready and empowered to write the next chapter of our life journey. I have seen women from our books bravely face their past, discover their true purpose, reclaim the power that had diminished over the years, and pivot onto an exciting new path. They launch a new business, up-level their existing business, or they ease into retirement with a renewed passion and fervor for life.

Embracing our story will change the direction of our next story and unveil our ultimate destiny.

Power to you and the story of your life!

*"For I know the plans I have for you,"* declares the Lord, *"plans to prosper you and not to harm you, plans to give you hope and a future."*

—Jeremiah 29:11

# Introduction

Here we are, publishing our twelfth book of the series featuring the inspirational stories of 17 women combined. (219 before this book) Unlike our previous books where I omitted my story to give others a chance to shine, I didn't this time. This book feels different for me. My life is different. Over the past 12 months, I've done a lot of soul searching, made a lot of monumental changes, and I will be sharing a bit about that in the pages to come.

Until then, I still want to share a bit about how our project came together.

My initial goal was to create one co-authored book, collecting stories from women I admired who were members of my organization, the Dynamic Professional Women's Network (DPWN). I knew how sharing my story in a similar book (compiled by a mentor of mine, Michelle Prince) had been transformational for me. I also knew how having a book to share in the business community gave me additional credibility, recognition, and exposure. What I didn't know was how these same stories would be just as transformational for the readers, as they related with one or more of the women who were willing to share their stories in such a vulnerable and authentic way.

I also had no way of knowing how working with these women would lead me down a path that would change "my" life forever...

I'm a natural connector. Many women are. I believe it's part of our DNA to connect people with other people or resources that can help them. I've often shared how my journey to build DPWN was not intentional. As an introvert, the last thing I wanted to do was build a business where I would have to frequently talk with new people... strangers. But thankfully, God knew better than I did what was best for me.

Now, 20 years later, our community has scaled down considerably due to the pandemic. We pivoted like so many other businesses. We tried a few things that worked and tried a few things that didn't work. We added more global members, supported the members who lost their businesses, and we continue to celebrate the local chapters that remained loyally dedicated to each other at a time when they needed each other the most. I am unsure what's around the corner for our network. However, I do know that thousands of women have grown their businesses through the relationships and connections they made in our community.

Our *Overcoming Mediocrity Project* is still going strong featuring an amazing lineup of epic women, we are in the third year of our podcast, and we are launching a new series under the Mastery Unleashed brand that will also include men's stories of strength, faith, and courage. All our books climbed to the #1 position on Amazon on the very first day of release, most of them in multiple categories. All of our stories are about having the confidence to believe in ourselves, even when those we love may not. They are about having the courage to do hard things, even when we don't want to. They are also about having an epic mindset through all of life's ups and downs.

Do you have a story of strength, faith, or courage? You can connect with us at: www.masteryunleashedcoaching.com

**Your Story**

What is your story?

Are you living your story, or are you living for someone else's story? Maybe you are living into your destiny. Or maybe you spend the majority of your time unhappily working for someone else, taking care of someone else, or doing something that does not create a fire in your soul. You're managing. However, you just can't seem to escape those pesty thought bubbles popping into your mind, reminding you that… "One of these days, it will be MY TURN."

**What if That Time Never Comes?**

The personal and professional development industry generates billions of dollars of revenue every year. According to www.marketresearch.com, the U.S. estimated market value for personal coaching was $955 million in 2015. In 2019 the estimated market value was $2.849 billion. That's a 21% increase over the 2015 estimate. The coaching industry remains strong, and, despite the economic downturn due to COVID-19, the industry will reach $17 billion by 2027. The great news is that for every one of those coaches, there are many people desperately searching for help.

I work with women and men who have reached a point in their lives, where they're finally ready to step into their destiny, own their story, and share their wisdom. People who don't think they have the skills to become a coach, but they know down deep in their gut that they CAN help people. They're considering stepping into a coaching or consulting role. However, they don't know where to start. Or they've been trying, and they're just not getting the results they desire (or frankly that they deserve).

If you just read that and felt a butterfly or two swirling around in your stomach, then maybe we should chat. I have a simple system that will provide you with the steps and support to build a profitable business as a coach, author, and speaker.

Hugs & Blessings,

Christie

# Table of Contents

Christie Ruffino: Tomorrow Isn't Promised ........................................... 1

Mara Stefan: Leaning In or Falling Out? We Need a New
Playbook for Women and Work .................................................. 17

Anastasia Paras: Designing Life on Your Terms ................................. 27

Dr. Susie Warden: Posture UP ............................................................ 35

Dr. Katrina Nguyen: From Poverty to Generosity ............................... 43

Kathryn D. Regganie: Shine Bright ..................................................... 55

Liz Orvis: I Get Knocked Down, But I Get Up Again ........................ 63

Tracy Eisenman: Get Your Sexy Back ................................................ 73

Kathleen Quink Shaw: Finding My Way: A Story of Love,
Learning, and Determination ........................................................ 79

Sheri Mills: Are You Ready for Your Bucket List? ............................ 87

Georgiana Danet: From Eating Rotten Tomatoes to
Being a Successful International Coach ....................................... 95

Barb Gabaldon: Storms of Adversity: The Quest
for Breakthrough .......................................................................... 105

Patricia Marie Larsen: The Many Triumphs of
Recovery and Healing .................................................................. 115

Faly Colaizzi: Discovering My Superpower ....................................... 121

Kim Falco: My Bucket ......................................................................... 129

Elizabeth Rose Daily-Izquierdo: It's Never Too Late…
    Even in The Storm ........................................................................135
Ruby Williams: Embracing A Life Beyond Alcohol..........................143

# Christie Ruffino

## *Tomorrow Isn't Promised*

Last week I was fine… Today, I have cancer.

Yesterday I was happy… Today, I am crushed by betrayal.

This morning, I held my mom's hand… Now she is gone.

I jolted awake. My heart still racing, my mind utterly confused by the experience I had just had. "I'm alive!" "What just happened?" The last thing I remember was looking at the clock for the hundredth time as sleep continued to evade me until the early morning hours. Suddenly, I was floating in a room above my family and friends as they were crying over my dead body. The Christie in that coffin wasn't an old woman who had lived a full life. I was looking at a version of me that was still young and vibrant, with many dreams still unlived. I was yelling at them, "*I'm alive, I'm alive*," but no matter how loud I screamed or how close I got, they could not hear me. I usually don't remember my dreams. However, this one was vivid, powerful, and unsettling.

As I collected my thoughts, the details of that dream did not fade away. In fact, they just became more and more real. I couldn't shake the experience, no matter how hard I tried. I fought to go back to sleep, but I just lay there, unaware of the subtle feeling of dread that would plague my thoughts the rest of the day.

The past few days had been amazing! I was on a professional development retreat with some incredible people at a beautiful Cabo San Lucas, Mexico resort. However, the dream that occurred on the last day of my journey terrified me. Was it a premonition? Should I be worried about my travels home? Or had the series of events from the past two years finally caught up with me… manifesting in a way that had me facing my own mortality? How could I know?

Was my subconscious tapped into something very important, something that I needed to listen to?

What does it mean?

What should I do?

Am I really going to die… soon?

I am not ready for the last chapter of my life to end. I still have big dreams and big plans! Most importantly, I still don't feel like I was fulfilling my true life's purpose.

**Going Through the Motions**

Many of us get up every morning and go through the motions of our day, believing that tomorrow is promised. We coast through life thinking that someday, one day, I will write that book, start that business, or follow my passions.

What if that day never comes?

And if it does… Are we brave enough to act?

So, there I was, on a beachside resort in Mexico, ready to be transformed. That was not the intention of the event I was at. However, it was MY intention because things needed to change. I've learned over the years how powerful our subconscious is. Over the past few days, I found myself way out of my comfort zone without even an inkling of how big of a shift was around the corner.

**The Silence of Isolation**

The Covid-19 pandemic created a monumental shift in everyone's lives. No one truly emerged from the claws of that beast unscathed. The challenges that I faced were much greater than those faced by many, and they continued long after "life as we knew it" returned back to normal.

I not only had to navigate the lockdown, the fear, and the uncertainty surrounding my mortality and that of those I loved. My mom was also dying. Every day, my heart ached, knowing how scared and alone she was feeling since her family could not be with her due to the quarantine regulations. I was blessed to have my children and grandkids living with me as we "sheltered at home." Needless to say, that joy didn't come without a boatload of complications.

I was also drowning in some serious debt. My physical well-being was declining, my business revenue came to a screeching halt, and I gained 20 pounds. Just when I thought things were starting to get better, WHAM!, I was knocked down again. The man I loved walked out of my life, ending our engagement without even letting me know or telling me why. He simply vanished without a word, leaving me dumbfounded.

Fear, loneliness, rejection, and isolation enveloped me once again, as silent and as heavy as a dark shadow. Self-pity and the feeling of failure had carved a home deep in my gut. This was not to mention the prickling feeling of hate. I hated my house, hated living in Illinois, hated men (I got over that quickly), hated the winter cold, hated many aspects of my life, and I felt like I was spiraling down into a bottomless pit of no return. The feeling was like a thick, heavy storm cloud that only I had the power to navigate.

So, when I learned about that southbound Mexico trip, I signed up immediately. I also decided to add a few extra weeks in Florida to escape the chaos that had become my life.

While I was there, I laughed, I cried, and I spent a lot of alone time reflecting on my life. There were so many aspects of my world that were upside down. I didn't see how things could ever be better. At the same time, I believed deep down in my soul that if I didn't make a change soon, my life would not end well.

**My Chrysalis**

Like a caterpillar, I began fabricating my chrysalis, embarking on my next journey of change. I was not sure how I was to emerge. However, I had to escape the insanity.

*"The definition of insanity is doing the same thing over and over and expecting different results."*

—Albert Einstein

I don't typically get strong messages from God to clarify my decisions and guide my actions. My faith is a strong ten. I also find comfort in knowing that His plan for my life is greater than even the biggest dreams I may have. However, I generally receive small nudges, notice small signs, and see events that confirm or disprove my prayers for guidance. This time, His message was loud and clear.

I was out of my element, surrounded by people who were thinking, living, and being much bigger than I could even imagine at the time. Embracing the fact that I was a little fish in an ocean of whales and sharks, I sat back and enjoyed the experience. I took notes, tore down my armor of vulnerability, and allowed myself to be open to expansion.

Help me, God!

I just want to serve. Please utilize my gifts, strengths, and passions to help others.

What do you want me to do?

I am broken, ready to be molded by your hands.

I am willing to leave behind the old. I am ready for the new.

What is your plan for me? I am open to change.

For me, the change was monumental.

It meant leaving behind everything I found comfort in.

It meant leaving my family.

It meant selling my home.

It meant re-inventing my business.

It meant getting out of my own way.

It meant getting really uncomfortable in order to find new comfort in an unknown path.

It meant not knowing the final destination.

I just had to keep my eyes focused on the next step.

An important lesson I learned years ago is that when riding a motorcycle, if you feel yourself going down, whatever you do, don't look down because you will crash. Always keep your eyes on the road ahead. If you do, you will have a better chance of keeping your bike upright and on a path to safety. You don't need to know the engineering behind how that happens. You just need to trust that your outcome will be much better than if you focus your sights on the impending crash zone.

This ride is very similar.

I am not certain of the engineering behind how I will get to my final destination.

I just know where I will arrive, and every step of the trip is bringing me closer to that beautiful result.

I broke free of the shell of my chrysalis, emerging from my past with color on my wings and courage in my heart.

At last, I was ready to follow my purpose. This was it. With God's hand on my shoulder, guiding me forward, I knew I'd forged the journey that would fulfill me and bring me joy.

**Your Chrysalis**

A major problem that I see in the world (besides slow drivers in the fast lane) is that too many women are still thinking small and not stepping into their power because they think, "Someday, one day," it will be my turn. They spend the majority of their life helping others accomplish their dreams. When it's finally their turn, they either don't know what they should do or they don't know how to do it in a way that will bring in a good income.

My desire for you is that you find the motivation, strength, and determination to break free of the shell of your chrysalis, emerging from your past with color on your wings and courage in your heart, ready to follow your purpose.

If you desire that, too, I want to share three keys to having a business that lights you up and makes you money.

**KEY #1: Reawaken Your Purpose**

The biggest fear I see with women who have decided to pursue their big mission in business comes from the fact that they've lost sight of their childlike hopes and dreams. They're also working on a business that does not follow their true purpose. They may think they are on the right track. However, deep down, they feel like they have to do the work BEFORE they can actually do the work.

The problem with this is…

- They feel unfulfilled and passionless, just going through the motions every day, not experiencing true joy.
- They are not living up to their God-given potential, wasting the precious gifts and experiences they've lived through.
- They are not making the impact they could, which would change the lives of many others that will ripple down through their future generations.

**Searching for a Sign**

Early on in my entrepreneurial journey, I thought I was pursuing my big mission. I recently got divorced, and as a way to get clients for the mortgage business I was in, I started a networking group. That little group evolved into a national organization with several chapters in many states and hundreds of members.

The irony of that season was that I was so focused on growing the group and helping them get more clients that I stopped getting my own clients. I lost interest in mortgages. I see now how that was the beginning of my mission awakening. However, I was too scared to dive in deep. I was dipping my toes in the shallow end of the pool because it was safe. I was watching colleagues and the women I would bring in to speak, and I was longing quietly inside to also share my message.

I truly enjoyed building the community and connection platform for the brilliant people in our organization to thrive. I believe that is one of the greatest gifts most women have. It is their desire and natural ability to create connections, build strong relationships, and care for those around them. While half of me embodied those strengths, the other half felt like there was something bigger I should be doing. I just didn't know what? But that's OK, I thought. I will figure it out one of these days. God will give me a sign. In the meantime, I stayed safe in my comfort zone and grew our organization way beyond my initial plan.

As the years rolled on, every time my mind drifted toward speaking, I banished those thoughts. I thought that I would have plenty of time to figure it out "someday one day." What I didn't realize then was that my lackadaisical timeline was, in essence, my way of creating a blind spot to stay small and safe.

Rachel Jayne Groover, in the book *Powerful and Feminine*, explains that our blind spots block us from seeing and feeling what we want. We drive down the road of life in the direction we think we should be going, with our true desires hidden from view. All while longing in our hearts for something else.

The problem with that way of thinking is that if we can't see and feel what we desire, we will never manifest it into reality. We will stay small and remain insignificant in the big game of life.

If you want to reawaken your purpose, this is what I suggest:

- Remove the blinders. Just take them off. You don't have to know what's next. Just recognize that you are seeing life through the lens of safety and start imagining what you would do if you knew you could not fail. Awareness is the first step in creating long and lasting change.

- Create your own urgency before something else does. Many of my clients create shifts because something significant happens to them that rips the blinders off and has them seeing things from a completely different perspective. They are forced to change. They don't like the experience at the time. However, in hindsight, they see the reason behind it. I sometimes feel that if we were to initiate change, certain things might not happen in our lives to force change. I may be naive in that thinking, but it has prompted me to make some uncomfortable changes that worked out for the best.

- Decide and take the first step. You don't have to know all of the steps necessary to get where you're going. You just need to decide and take the first step. Once you do that, your Reticular Activating System (RAS) will expand your thinking and allow you to become aware of bigger and better resources necessary for future steps, as needed.

**KEY #2: Step Into Your Genius Zone**

The biggest frustration that I see with women who have decided to pursue their big mission in business, is that they don't know how to tap into the power of their genius zone. Heck, most of them don't even know what their genius zone is.

Should they volunteer? Should they switch careers? Should they start a business? That may sound exciting, but how do they go about that in a way that they won't fail? The number of questions that can swirl around in their heads is endless. If they do decide to embark on the entrepreneurial journey, they try to figure out what path to take on their own and wind up taking the long, frustrating, and expensive road to failure.

The problem with this is…

- They don't tap into their genius zone and try to build a business that is way out of alignment. It doesn't connect with their audience because it doesn't connect with themself on a soul level.
- They are dabbling in a little bit of everything instead of landing on a core business focus that gets their clients great results and attracts people who will pay top dollar for their help.
- They are frustrated and much too busy trying to chase down clients instead of attracting them powerfully and serving them authentically.

**Dreams of a Child**

What do you want to do when you grow up, Christie? I reflected on that question several times during my "adult" life. There I was, all grown up, feeling like I was five again in my little pink leotard and tights, wanting to be a ballerina.

Then, one day, about ten years into turning my baby networking group into a full-blown association serving hundreds of women with a not-for-profit arm, someone asked me to share my story.

*"No way!"* I quickly responded.

For as far back as I can remember, my shy, introverted personality commanded my experience of life. I disliked large crowds and making new friends. I struggled to enjoy conversing with new people, so I avoided it like the plague. Always hyperaware of myself, I focused too much on wondering whether people liked me or if I said the right things, instead of even caring about them and what they had to say.

So, the thought of sharing my story was downright scary!

I would be vulnerable. What if the people who read my story hated it? What if they hated me? *"Who wants to hear my story anyways?"* I confidently asked.

I didn't think she would have an answer that would sway me. How could she?

Then she replied, *"All of the women who are knee-deep in the mess you dredged out of and need a little inspiration to come out on the other side to become successful in business."*

What could I say to that?

My fast "NO" turned into a fearful "yes." I never looked back.

Not only did that exercise grow me personally, but I also witnessed my business grow faster. New opportunities came to me because they saw my book or read my story.

Saying yes to that question allowed me to discover my genius zone of helping other women clarify, write, and share their stories for more impact.

When you have the courage to step into your genius zone, you will break through to unparalleled heights of productivity, impact, and life satisfaction.

What is your genius zone?

How can you bring forth your genius in a way that serves you and do it in a way that others will pay you to serve them?

If you want to discover your genius zone, take a moment to answer these questions:

- What "non-work" things do you love to do so much, that you can do them for hours on end without getting tired or bored?
- What "work" things do you love to do so much, that you can do them for hours on end without getting tired or bored?
- What work things do you do that produce the highest ratio of satisfaction and results to the amount of time spent doing it?
- What is your unique and priceless ability that may not be obvious, and when you drill down into your list of abilities, you'll find it to be something that most people don't possess?

**KEY #3: Create an Unstoppable Business**

The biggest challenge I see with women who have decided to pursue their big mission in business, is that they are not making significant money consistently. They jump into the coaching/consulting space without the proper systems in place that will leverage their time, talents, and financial treasures.

The problem with this is…

- They are working tirelessly with their private clients at low rates. Regardless of how rewarding that is, the only way to make more is to work more.
- They've created a collection of courses and low-ticket programs. However, only a few people have ever bought them.
- They've tried many tactics to get more clients. However, none of them seem to be working. They are not ready or willing to run a complicated program launch.
- They are SICK AND TIRED of paying for programs that over-sell and under-deliver!

One of my clients, we'll call her Karen, came to me recently because she wanted a more consistent income. She was having some great months. However, she also had too many months where she had to dip into her savings just to get the bills paid.

She had an extensive career in the medical field and skills that could help a lot of different ailments. At the same time, her daughter had Crohn's Disease, and she went on a quest to help her holistically. Because she was passionate about that focus, we niched her business down to that one area. We were able to sharpen her message to start attracting more clients.

In doing so, her business model is now simpler, people are now referring more clients to her, and we started implementing my scale-back process. She now only schedules appointments and serves her clients on the first three weeks of every month, leaving the fourth open to travel, to be creative, and to spend more time with her grandkids.

Karen is now unstoppable!

If you want to create an UNSTOPPABLE business, I invite you to join our team of women who are on the same path.

EPIC Mastery is a Pay-per-results group mentorship program designed to ensure you launch, sell, and scale your six-figure premium program in six to nine months.

Do you really want to reach the end of your time having not chased what you truly wanted, what you were called to do? It is more than that. While it's fun to chase our dreams, it's soul-fulfilling when we can actually catch them.

So, let me ask you this, *"What would you do with the rest of your life if you had $1 million in the bank and you knew you cannot fail?"*

If you want to have a profitable business pursuing your purpose, let's chat.

Learn more at: www.Epic-Mastery.com

# Christie Lee Ruffino

Christie Lee Ruffino is a serial entrepreneur, podcast host, international speaker, and best-selling author with 14 books. She has been featured on Inc.com, WGN Radio, and The Morning Blend on NBC TV. She is a Certified John Maxwell Coach and has studied under a long list of business icons such as Bob Burg, Jack Canfield, and Larry Winget.

Christie is an avid reader, a serial smart-ass, and a proud grandma of the two most adorable kids ever!!!! (And she has thousands of photos to prove it.) She swears she will NEVER skydive but is addicted to triple-digit speeds down open country roads on her Harley.

She has over three decades of business experience, built three six-figure businesses, and has worked with over three thousand women, helping them increase their business revenue through clarity, collaboration, and increased visibility.

All this experience has come together in a way that now serves her clients at the highest level. As a Profitize Your Purpose™ Coach, Christie guides entrepreneurs through her process to harness the power of STORY, SYSTEMS, and COMMUNITY to build a more dynamic brand, attract more clients, and make more money.

Christie Lee Ruffino
Mastery Unleashed Coaching
630-336-3773
Christie@ChristieRuffino.com
www.ChristieRuffino.com
www.MasteryUnleashedCoaching.com

## Profitize Your Purpose Powerpack

The ultimate resource bundle to embrace your big mission and have a profitable business that lights you up.

Includes:

- Profitize Your Purpose Micro-Course and Action Guide: To become crystal clear about your dream business so you can bring it to fruition directly and powerfully.

- EPIC Mastery Roadmap: To walk you through the step-by-step process to launch, sell, and scale a 6-figure Lux Group Coaching Program™ that guarantees EPIC results for your clients.

- EPIC Business Checklist: To identify what must be done to STOP trading hours for dollars and chasing down clients and START spending your time and money on strategies that get EPIC results.

BONUS: Living My Purpose Audio Affirmations MP3 File to ensure you don't stray, get overwhelmed, or become distracted.

www.ProfitizeYourPurposeGift.com

# Mara Stefan

## *Leaning In or Falling Out? We Need a New Playbook for Women and Work*

According to estimates from the World Bank, 27 million women left the global workforce as a result of the Covid-19 pandemic. These departures affected all sectors of work (including jobs in retail, hospitality, and entertainment) and accounted for roughly 34% of the estimated 80 million global workers who were forced to leave their jobs during the pandemic.

A 2022 report by the US Bureau of Labor Statistics confirms that the percentage of women participating in the labor force (working or looking for work) has fallen to **56.2 percent**, the lowest rate since 1987, and nearly four percentage points below the peak of 60 percent in 1999. Women still need new ways of working and having support both at work and at home, with many deeming *flexibility* the new currency in this new world of work.

The pandemic has also shown us just how fragile our lives are. It has realigned many women's priorities, my own included, in this new working world. The balancing act we had to perform when schools were closed, when parents were isolated from other family members, and when the workforce went almost completely digital in a matter of weeks, changed everything about the way the world operated, especially for women. The obstacles women faced in the workplace existed long before Covid. However, the pandemic has shined a harsh light on those realities.

As I was growing up in the 1970s, like many of my generation, I was a fan of the Carpenters. The iconic song, *"Rainy Days and Mondays"* was one of their most popular songs. It still creates a melancholy feeling whenever I hear it. It also represents the way I have continued to feel about Mondays, since my mother's passing on Monday, April 29, 2013.

It's taken me this last decade to truly appreciate how her death provided me with a deepening understanding of love, loss, and the inevitable transformation that time has brought me. It has also reshaped my understanding of what my career means to me, and what I need to be successful in the work I do.

I've been fortunate to have had a professional career that has allowed me to travel the world, own a business, interact with top executives, and make a late-career pivot to the corporate world of IT services and professional staffing. What a great opportunity it has been to work in the industry, as I write this chapter and future books on the same topic. All of these experiences have only fueled my passion for developing a platform to help women in the world of work navigate the gender gap, the leadership gap, the lack of diversity and inclusion gap, talent scarcity, quiet quitting, quiet hiring, and all other "gaps" and "quiets" that haven't yet been identified.

In 2013, while I was mourning the loss of my mother, another notable event occurred. Sheryl Sandberg, the former COO at Facebook (now Meta), had just released her manifesto, *Lean In: Women, Work, and the Will to Lead.* She wrote about the leadership ambition gap and encouraged the next generation of women to "lean in" to working and chasing their career ambitions, while balancing their personal lives at home. She talked about the dwindling numbers of women in top leadership roles as her career progressed and thanked the several male mentors that helped her along the way.

Her personal lessons were interesting and provided guidance on dealing with imposter syndrome, fake-it-til-you-feel-it syndrome, and other encouraging career suppositions. My personal favorite, the tiara syndrome, describes the expectations placed on girls and women to wear a metaphorical tiara and to be perfect in all areas of their lives despite the anxiety, stress, and overwhelming sense of guilt felt for not living up to these impossible standards. This syndrome has impacted me for most of my adult working life.

**But That Was Then, This Is Now.**

Sheryl's belief that we should all maximize our careers by chasing the top leadership positions while taking care of children, parents, and partners at home was nothing short of aspirational. As the world returns to a post-pandemic normal, the world of work has enabled millions of workers the opportunity to work remotely and in new hybrid setups. What hasn't changed in the decade since her book was published, is the bro culture of Silicon Valley. This has only made hiring and retaining women in the field of technology, for example, an even greater challenge. According to a study by the Center for Talent Innovation, 45% of women in science, engineering, and technology fields leave their jobs within the first year, compared to only 31% of men.

**How Does My Story Relate?**

Back in 2013, while Sheryl Sandberg was touting *Lean In*, I was barely keeping it together as a sandwich-generation mother and daughter. I was lucky to get through the day with dinner on the table, laundry started (but rarely finished), and before my mom's death, making sure she was taking her medications, all while attempting to work from home when needed. Does this sound familiar? As a single working mother, every day was organized chaos, to say the least. If I hadn't had the flexibility of running my own business, any employer would have had good reason to fire me for the time I needed to manage all the madness. It was very easy to ignore my own needs, as I sought to take care of everyone else's.

**Cue The Tiara**

What do women want now, and how can they navigate the considerable challenges in front of them? For a better understanding of changing workplace attitudes — let's highlight several areas where we must do better for the next generation in the workforce.

**Equity Versus Equality**

Women continue to be underrepresented in leadership positions. According to a 2021 report by LeanIn.org and McKinsey & Company, women make up only 28% of senior vice president roles, 21% of C-suite roles, and just 8% of CEO positions at Fortune 500 companies. This lack of representation is having significant impacts on workplace culture and policies, as well as on the opportunities available to women at all levels of the organization.

According to a 2021 report by the National Women's Law Center, women have lost more than five million jobs since the start of the pandemic, and women of color have been particularly hard hit. The report also notes that women are more likely to be essential workers and frontline healthcare workers, putting them at greater risk of exposure to the virus. These disparities highlight the need for policies that address the unique challenges women face in the workplace and support their economic security and well-being.

Equity in the workplace is especially important for women, who have historically faced discrimination and bias in hiring, pay, and promotion. Women continue to face challenges in the workplace, and achieving equity remains an ongoing struggle.

The gender pay gap persists, with women earning less than men for comparable work. In the United States, according to data from the National Women's Law Center, women earn just 82 cents for every dollar earned by men. The gap is even wider for women of color, with Black women earning just 63 cents and Latina women earning just 55 cents for every dollar earned by white, non-Hispanic men. This pay disparity can have long-term effects on women's earning potential and retirement savings, as well as on their overall financial security.

Women are more likely than men to face harassment and discrimination in the workplace. According to a 2018 report by the Equal Employment Opportunity Commission (EEOC), nearly one-third of all sexual harassment charges filed with the agency come from the hospitality, retail, and healthcare industries, which are often dominated by women workers. Women who report harassment or discrimination may also face retaliation or other negative consequences, making it difficult for them to advance in their careers.

**Microaggressions in the Workplace**

Microaggressions have had a particularly detrimental impact on women in the workplace. Women are more likely than men to experience microaggressions related to gender, including comments or actions that minimize their expertise, stereotype their behavior, or objectify them, making it difficult for women to establish themselves as leaders or experts in their fields.

This can make it difficult for women to establish credibility or to be taken seriously in their roles, which can limit their opportunities for advancement.

When women experience comments or actions that are demeaning or disrespectful, it can create a sense of discomfort or even fear in the workplace and contribute to a hostile work environment. According to a 2018 report by the National Women's Law Center, nearly one in three women have experienced sexual harassment at work. The majority of women who experience harassment report that it affects their mental health and job performance.

Microaggressions also contribute to the gender pay gap. When women are treated as less competent or valuable than their male colleagues, they may be more likely to receive lower pay or fewer opportunities for advancement.

It must also be considered that enduring this type of behavior can lead to higher levels of stress and burnout among women in the workplace.

Microaggressions can lead to a lack of diversity and inclusion in the workplace. When women feel that they are not valued or respected, they are less likely to participate in workplace initiatives or to share their perspectives and ideas. This can limit the diversity of thought and experience within the organization, which can hinder innovation and growth. A lack of diversity can make it difficult for companies to appeal to a diverse customer base or to effectively address the needs of diverse communities.

## Ageism is Alive and Well in the Workforce

Ageism, or discrimination based on age, can have a significant impact on women in the workforce. Women, particularly those over the age of 50, are more likely than men to experience ageism in the workplace, which can affect their job prospects, career advancement, and financial stability.

The odds get worse for a woman the older she becomes. According to a 2019 report by the National Women's Law Center, women over the age of 55 are more likely than men to experience long-term unemployment.

When women are seen as "too old" for certain positions or roles, they may be passed over for promotions or opportunities for professional development. AARP reports that three in five workers over the age of 45 have seen or experienced age discrimination in the workplace. A total of 92% of those who have experienced age discrimination say that it is common.

A woman's age can also contribute to the gender pay gap. According to data from the National Women's Law Center, women over the age of 65 earn just 80 cents for every dollar earned by men in the same age group. This gap is even wider for women of color, with Black women over the age of 65 earning just 68 cents for every dollar earned by white, non-Hispanic men in the same age group.

Companies must do better to combat ageism in the workplace, promoting diversity and inclusion at all levels of the organization and valuing the contributions of workers of all ages.

## Navigating the Queen Bee Syndrome

The *"Queen Bee Syndrome"* is a phenomenon in which women in positions of power treat other women harshly and, in some cases, undermine them. These women may feel threatened by other women who are trying to advance in their careers, and they may attempt to maintain their own power by sabotaging or belittling their female colleagues. The term *"queen bee"* comes from the idea that these women have succeeded in male-dominated industries by adopting stereotypically masculine traits and rejecting feminine traits, and they may view other women as a threat to their success.

This behavior is detrimental to women in the workforce because it creates a hostile work environment and can make it more difficult for women to succeed. Women who experience this kind of behavior may be less likely to speak up, seek mentorship, or ask for help, which can hinder their career advancement. When women are pitted against each other, it reinforces stereotypes and makes it harder to achieve gender equality in the workplace. The queen bee syndrome undermines the principles of collaboration and support that are crucial to creating a work environment in which everyone can thrive. It is important to address this issue by promoting a culture of inclusivity and support, and by encouraging women to lift each other up rather than tearing each other down.

## Making the Case for the Four-Day Workweek

The four-day workweek is becoming increasingly popular among employers, especially those looking to attract and retain women in the workforce. Research has shown that a four-day workweek can offer numerous benefits to both employers, while employers can reap the rewards of improved employee engagement and productivity. A recent study conducted by the University of Oxford found that employees who worked four days per week reported higher levels of job satisfaction, better work-life balance, and improved performance. The study also found that these employees were more likely to stay with their employer for a longer period of time.

## Mental Health and Beating Burnout

According to a 2018 report by the American Psychological Association, women are more likely than men to report experiencing chronic stress related to work, with factors such as discrimination and gender bias contributing to this stress.

Several steps can be taken to combat mental health issues and burnout among women in the workforce:

- **Promote Work-Life Balance:** Employers can help prevent burnout by encouraging work-life balance. This can include flexible working hours, remote work, and offering paid time off. Employees who feel that they can balance work and personal responsibilities are less likely to experience burnout.

- **Create a Supportive Work Environment:** Employers can create a supportive work environment by offering employee assistance programs, mental health resources, and promoting open communication. A culture of support and respect can help employees feel more comfortable seeking help, if they are struggling with mental health issues.

- **Address Inequality:** Women are often subjected to sexism and gender-based discrimination in the workforce, which can lead to feelings of stress, anxiety, and burnout. Employers can address these issues by creating inclusive policies and practices, providing anti-discrimination training, and promoting diversity and inclusion.

- **Encourage Self-Care:** Employers can encourage self-care by providing resources and promoting activities, such as meditation, exercise, and stress reduction techniques. Encouraging healthy habits can help employees manage stress and maintain their mental health.

- **Offer Mental Health Benefits:** Employers can offer mental health benefits, such as counseling services and mental health days. These benefits can help employees access the resources they need to manage their mental health.

While we've come a long way in helping women navigate the world of work, there are many more miles to go before we reach parity. Until we do, the world of work will continue to be unevenly distributed, and eventually, the talent shortage will become a talent crisis.

# Mara Stefan

Mara has spent most of her more than 25-year career helping companies and executives establish thought leadership positions within their industries. Currently, she is the VP of Global Insights for ManpowerGroup, one of the world's leading talent advisory and solutions companies. The firm employs more than 30,000 people in 75 countries who are focused on transforming the world of work. She previously led global thought leadership for The Adecco Group prior to joining ManpowerGroup.

Mara also directed strategic marketing and communications at Cognizant's Center for the Future of Work. Mara founded and oversaw Emerge Public Relations, where she provided marketing, public relations, and strategic counsel to many Global 1000 organizations. Prior to Emerge PR, she spent nine years at The Horn Group, a Silicon Valley PR powerhouse, rising to General Partner in charge of the firm's Boston office.

Prior to joining The Horn Group, Mara handled PR at Borland Software Corp. — the PC software firm co-founded by maverick entrepreneur Philippe Khan. She has also overseen strategic partnerships with many organizations, including The World Economic Forum, TED, The Nantucket Project, and Thinkers50, among others. She earned a Bachelor of Arts in Communications with a Minor in Journalism from Stephen F. Austin University.

Mara Stefan
VP of Global Insights
ManpowerGroup
476 King Street
Cohasset, MA 02025
781-771-6911
MaraJStefan@outlook.com
www.LinkedIn.com/in/MaraStefan

# Anastasia Paras

## *Designing Life on Your Terms*

There I was, trembling with fear as I waited backstage to be called out to share my story in front of thousands. I could hardly catch my breath. I was praying that I didn't pass out. What deep emotional scars might I leave with my little girl seeing her mom get carried off stage in a stretcher because she hyperventilated and passed out?

A mountain of fearful thoughts came crashing down on my head at once. I was in a full-blown panic. I was asked to share my story of how I successfully rose through fear in order to facilitate growth. Yet, here I was, confronting yet another fear… my fear of public speaking. Oh, the irony. Just when I thought there was no way I could do this and I was scouting the exits to make a break for it, my mentor put his hands on my shoulders and reminded me that what I was there to do, wasn't about me. This is about a message that I needed to deliver to help others. I knew that I had been overthinking and realized I had it backward. At that moment, I made the shift. That gave me the courage to step out of my comfort zone into that moment to serve others and deliver the message.

**How Did I Get Here?**

Several years earlier, I had been with a company for eight years. I worked hard and made it into the top 2% of that company by building a large and very productive team. Regardless of how "successful" we were, I began feeling that something was still missing. Do you know that "wake up excited" feeling you have when you're aligned and living your purpose? Well, I was not in that place. I had lost that spark. I continued to show up, and no one would've noticed, but I knew I felt more like I was just going through the motions instead of making an impact.

**My Lightbulb Moment...**

We all find a way to keep going. I did too. Days turned into weeks. However, I kept hearing that voice that I was meant for more. We all have that gut instinct, spirit, and intuitive self that knows if you're on course or off. Whether you call it God, your soul or intuition, or you call it the universe... whatever you call it, mine kept talking. And the more I ignored it, the louder it got. It kept telling me that my "this" wasn't it, that I was meant for so much more. That life holds every promise I could imagine and dream of if only I would listen, trust it, embrace and believe the whisperings, and act on them. Only then would I find myself in harmony and integrity with my true, purposeful self. It would require a leap of faith. However, if I followed my heart, everything I needed would show up.

Here I was, on stage, talking about how I was able to rise through all the fear, doubt, and noise to step out into the unknown. I talked about how I left a career that no longer served me or allowed me to serve others at my highest potential. The message was that it's never too late to start over. Growth happens when we push through fear, and that fear is a liar. Fear tries to hold us back from living our best lives, selling out for comfort rather than pursuing thrilling. We must identify and push through this fear and doubt found in limiting beliefs and move into love and abundance to find and live our God-given potential.

I got a standing ovation! A pregnant lady even came up to me in tears and told me how much she connected with my story and that she was so grateful I shared it. Her tears could have been the pregnancy hormones. However, I chose to believe that I personally impacted her.

*It turns out... I'm a GREAT public speaker.*

## My Second Light Bulb Moment...

If hindsight is 20/20, then my vision was crystal clear. I remember that plane ride home from that speech with my toddler very well. She goes everywhere with me. She is my miracle. I had her at 43. I have designed my life AROUND her so I don't miss out on those important moments. Having her along to see her Mama in another light has been very important. I have been very blessed to be able to do so. I have also created a career out of helping others design life on THEIR terms, whatever that means to them.

It hit me as I sat on the plane, replaying the moments, reflecting on the experience, and recalling all the positive feedback. It was like a ton of bricks. That voice again. I can talk the talk, but how could I continue to authentically teach and inspire others to design life on their terms when I wasn't walking the walk in my personal life? Ouch! I had risen professionally. However, here I was again, feeling stuck personally, wondering if I had the courage to start my life over. I needed to step out of the shadows that had been dimming me and allow my light to shine. To choose ME. Doubts again filled my head. What would people think? What impact would this have on the people around me? I mean, it wasn't horrible. There were people I knew who had it much worse. Maybe this was as good as it was going to get for me. Self-doubt is exactly what fear places in our heads to keep us "safely" where we are, which is not safe at all.

It has been my experience that when we contemplate change, we initially resist. Knowing something is one thing. Living something is altogether different. Knowing is not living. It's also not thriving. I knew what to do. However, could I summon the courage to change everything? This wasn't just for me. I owed it to my daughter as well as myself to be better and to do better, to set a better example. I needed to be stronger than my fear.

I knew what I didn't want. I imagined what I did want. I considered the first steps I would need to take and the kind of people I would need around me. I stacked these up against the fear that would try to hold me back and decided it was time to break through to change.

I went back to the same three steps I used to rise through fear professionally and applied it.

**STEP ONE: *Quiet the Noise, Get Clear, and Identify the Fear.***

For me, it was fear of failure, judgment, the unknown, of starting over, of being a single mother, and of the impact it would have on my daughter.

Even the thought of it triggered that scared little 7-year-old girl who stood over my grandfather's grave while my mother told me what I knew was coming: that she and my dad were getting divorced. All those feelings and thoughts came rushing back. Was it my fault? Could I have been better? There was fear of the unknown. I didn't want my daughter to feel even a tiny bit of what I went through. I stayed longer because of that. However, then I got clear that staying in an unhealthy, unloving marriage would be way worse than leaving. I didn't want my unhealthy relationship with her father to be the barometer of what she used as she got older. With that thought, things came into focus.

**STEP TWO: *Embrace the Pain as It's Part of the Process.***

Sit with the pain and embrace it. You must know that it's temporary and part of the process. You must extend yourself some grace. Allow yourself to feel. Know that it *is* ok to *not* be ok. Sometimes, you need to pause and sit in the yuck in order to learn and grow.

I sat through a lot of pain. I did a lot of mourning. I had to come to the realization that the reality of my situation was so much different than the story I was telling myself. Sometimes, no matter how hard you try, things don't work. I had to allow myself the space to feel things that I hadn't allowed myself to feel. I felt the pain, failure, shame, and defeat. I felt it all.

I had waited until I was almost 43 to get married. I never really put a lot into the idea of marriage. However, I thought it would be better when my daughter was born to be married. So, two months before she was born, I married her father. There were red flags long before we even married. However, I thought to myself that all relationships have problems. I kept going through the motions, thinking that was best for my daughter. I wanted to protect her and ultimately avoid the pain I went through as a child of divorce. Once I allowed myself to sit in that pain and to gain clarity on what the truth really was, I was able to rise through the yuck and be crystal clear on what needed to be done.

**STEP THREE:** *Make a Plan and Tighten Your Circle.*

You have identified the fear. You have sat in pain. Now, it's time to take action. Remember, you are the sum of the people you keep company with. Make sure that you surround yourself with people who fully support you. A lot of times, this means you will have to tighten up your circle and maybe let some people go. As you are restructuring your life, you must reevaluate some people in it.

My circle became smaller and tighter. I made sure that the company I kept had my best interests in mind and that they understood the plan and supported it. All the rest was just noise. I can hear and appreciate what others say and think. There is a big difference between caring and defining.

*"When we stop caring what people think, we lose the capacity to connect. When we become defined by what people think, we lose the courage to become vulnerable."*

—Brené Brown

People will gossip, will create their version of the truth, and will come around offering to help when all they want is gossip. Let them talk, whisper, and tell whatever story they want. They do not define you. You do. Misery loves company, but my friend, you are choosing better, so stand in that truth.

Dream it.

Plan it.

Own it.

Believe it.

Live it.

Love it.

Here I am, at almost 50, starting over as a single mama to a six-year-old. I can say that my decisions have made all the difference in living life on my terms. I have never been more prepared, felt more supported and loved by true friends and family, and was never more open to all the possibilities and more excited for the future. Never hold on to the past at the expense of your future. Life is lived in moments. Present moments.

May you have trust in knowing that you are much stronger than you believe you are or could ever imagine, that it's truly never too late to start over, and that there are beautiful new beginnings on the other side of fear. You are worthy of all the greatness that was created for you.

The time to claim it is NOW!

You deserve to live the life you love on your terms.

# Anastasia Paras

Anastasia is a super-connector and a possibility-creating powerhouse. She brings imagination, creativity, action, and consistency to everything she does. For the past ten years, she has designed a life most would envy. She has mastered a process, and in doing so, she has been able to build multiple businesses, several into seven figures. She is bright, funny, playful, and has great leadership discipline and instincts. She has coached, trained, inspired, and led big teams to sales success. Her superpower is connecting people with a passion to opportunities that build an income, all while designing their lives on their terms. She helps people start earning income immediately while moving in the direction of their dreams. She has developed a proven process. She has done this work thousands of times over the years. She was managing to accomplish all of this as a single mom, of a beautiful, high-energy daughter. Although busy running her own successful business life, she is also managing the demands of her busy child actor daughter, who is cast on the world's most-watched television show. Anastasia will tell you that her greatest title, that of Mom, she earned in her early 40s after a miraculous IVF process. In fact, she and her daughter, Sophia, were recently featured on the cover of GO in January of 2023, sharing her incredible story. This busy mama and social media influencer, is living her life on purpose, with joy, and the freedom to choose where she wants to be, without the need to ask for permission. She is practicing exactly what she preaches, by living her life her way. If you are ready to make the move to take ownership of your life, you are going to want to know what Anastasia knows.

Anastasia Paras
Life Designer
RiseThroughWithMe@gmail.com
www.Facebook.com/Anastasia.Paras
www.BossLadyBio.com/ParasGirls
www.Instagram.com/TheAnastasiaParas

# Dr. Susie Warden

## *Posture UP*

*When your life is coming apart at the seams...*
*you "POSTURE UP"...*
*stand straight and walk boldly through the finish line!*

As I sit in this 100-year-old, musty, hot, sweaty attic with hundreds of containers of patient records, I wonder to myself... How will I survive this ordeal? I read the legal subpoena requesting the last seven years of patient files. Am I going to lose everything because of this greedy person wanting money from me? Will I be able to afford my $500/ hr. lawyers to prove my innocence through this? Will I be able to keep my practices, pay my employees, AND maintain our family expenses for my five kids? I really have no choice; they want this discovery. I have nothing to hide, so let us find what they are asking for, continue to do what I do (help my patients get healthy), and pray for the best!!

When you find that you are getting attacked from every direction, how can you gather the energy to stand straight and walk boldly through it?

Life has extreme challenges. When you are in the middle of one, how do you continue without falling apart and giving up? This is my story; you may have one of your own! We all have that time in our lives when it is EASIER to just give up. However, easier is NEVER better!! Stand strong, hold your ground, and know that you are stronger than you think you are!

**How It Started**

I grew up in Montana with two brothers. My parents stressed arduous work, doing your absolute best, and NEVER GIVING UP! I excelled in sports, waited tables, met people, took names, and created relationships through college and into my mid-20s! I met the love of my life, got married, had two boys, and we decided that to have our future in our own hands, I would go to chiropractic school. We could open clinics, train people, change lives, and duplicate the system! Chiropractic school was no walk in the park. It was a five-year program crammed into 3½ years, with three kids and sometimes eight tests/week. However, we knew that it was just time, and it had an end! We would get through it and begin our life helping others!

Our plan was unfolding perfectly. We had another baby and hired a consulting company to coach us exactly how to hire, train, and bill for medical doctors, physical therapists, massage therapists, and chiropractors. We followed the plan, trained our employees, and helped our patients isolate the cause of their pain. We taught them how to eliminate it, keep it away, and live as a better version of themselves!

**When Things Changed**

All was going as planned until I hired an employee who wanted money from me. She accused me of what she thought was wrong, as she was just graduating from chiropractic school. I knew I was not wrong and decided to start a seven-year court case in which the only winners were my attorneys! Our monthly attorney bills were unbearable!! To keep up, we had to consolidate offices and downsize our house, while knowing it was the right thing to do! Throughout the seven years, I realized that POSTURING UP (the ability to ACT like I was ON TOP OF THE WORLD with a smile on my face, shoulders back, and matching energy!!) created the energy I needed to fight the good fight. I had to do it to get through and beyond this nightmare! Whether I felt great or NOT, I pulled my shoulders back and created my own energy!!

**This Is How I Had to Get Through This Nightmare...**

I opened offices, trained more employees, continued to help patients find a better, pain-free life, and tried to keep up with attorney bills with a smile on my face! Every time my attorney called, my heart would sink. There was more discovery needed and more bills to pay. I had four boys at this point in my life. I was at every basketball, football, and baseball game, preparing healthy food, and attempting to be the best mom/doctor without quitting it all!! I read personal development books to try to keep my mind right. I learned that I had to wake up every day, tell myself that it was GOING TO BE A GREAT DAY, and found that by pulling my shoulders back and standing straight with a smile on my face, I had a better chance of creating positive energy, than doing what I really wanted to do, which was to stay in bed and cry!! I was worried about what was next, how much I could stand, what would happen if I could not afford the bills, and whether I should just give up. If I did give up, then what? Nonetheless, I had patients to see and needed to muster up the energy while this nightmare unfolded. I had no choice other than to posture up and get through it!!

**Why Posture?**

Posture is at the root of each aspect of life! Neurologic input to every cell in your entire body relies on the function of each vertebral joint throughout the spine. In turn, depending on various other aspects as well, your spine functions best as posture is as close to perfect as it can be! We are upright beings, and as time has evolved, trauma has ensued. Posture can be the cause of pain and dysfunction. With forward head carriage, the pressure and weight that is put on the neck, middle back, lower back, and all the way to the hamstrings and calves can cause everything from headaches and shoulder pain to lower back problems and tight hamstrings and calves. For every patient who comes into our offices complaining about pain, POSTURE is the #1 cause!! We begin working on EASY exercises and stretches that, if done daily, are life-changing!

**Posture Creates Energy**

Holding the head back, shoulders back, chest out, and walking with SWAG (SWAG is the feeling you have when you are on top of the world. You look and feel great! Sometimes SWAG has to be faked!!) will create an energy that WILL GET YOU THROUGH anything. Energy OUT = energy back IN!! Now, how you really feel, at times, you may want to stay in bed, not excited to get dressed and help people, or be the motivator. You may show up with your head and shoulders forward, presenting with a LOW ENERGY shuffle, which will never attract anything good!! So here is the question… Will you stand up straight and pull those shoulders back with ENERGY or the LOW ENERGY shuffle? It is totally up to you!

**I Chose SWAG**

I could not let this situation slow me down! There were too many patients and people who needed to hear what I went through and how I used POSTURE to get through the nightmare. I did not let ANYONE steal my dreams or goals or keep me from helping others get through their challenges.

This was my story and how I chose to get through it. You may have a similar nightmare that could cause you to want to quit, take yourself out of the game, or just give up. I encourage you to use my story and choose NOT to quit! Posture UP, shoulders back, and walk boldly through this time in your life. It WILL be better. You will be better AND stronger!

# Dr. Susie Warden

Growing up in MT allowed Dr. Susie to enjoy an active lifestyle that she wanted to continue throughout her college days and career. She pursued a bachelor's degree in Exercise Physiology and graduated from Arizona State University with plans to help people change their lives through health and fitness.

She continued her passion for health and helping people as she started her own fitness consulting business at 22 years old in Boca Raton, Florida. She consulted corporations to help get their employees healthier, therefore saving 100's of thousands of dollars in insurance premiums. She became acutely aware that there were A LOT of people who needed more than fitness consulting! One day, she met a young woman who was a chiropractor, and this conversation changed the trajectory of Dr. Susie's life.

*"I saw this chiropractor help people in ACUTE and chronic pain, and without the use of drugs or surgery, totally change their lives! I decided right then to pursue a degree in chiropractic and never turned back!"*

After finishing the prerequisites needed before starting her chiropractic education, Dr. Susie, Chris, her husband, and two children packed up and moved from Florida to Chicago, where she attended the National College of Chiropractic in Lombard. It was 1994 when she started the program; in 1997, Dr. Susie earned her Doctor of Chiropractic, had two more boys, and has been practicing her love of natural healthcare ever since!

She and her husband knew that they would raise the five boys, open multiple offices, and train other chiropractors and healthcare practitioners to work together and help people change their lives to a healthier version. They have been phenomenally successful in all aspects, with a few life-changing challenges, for the past 30 years!

Dr. Susie's passion is to coach and encourage people, whether in the office or in packed conference rooms, to decide to be a better version of themselves. As a health coach and motivational speaker, she encourages people, through sharing her own life challenges, never to give up on their passion to be better! She likes to do one-on-one sessions with people and encourages them to get out of their comfort zones so they can live the life of their dreams.

She uses her degrees, years of experience, and personal stories to encourage people NOT to settle for less than their dream life! Giving back to her community is also one of Dr. Susie's passions by speaking to students, professional organizations, women's groups, and churches. You can find her in Wheaton volunteering at various events and helping people in the community.

Dr. Susie Warden

Advanced Healthcare Associates

416 E Roosevelt Road, #107

Wheaton, IL 60187

630-260-1300

www.Facebook.com/Susie.Warden.73

www.Instagram.com/DrSusieAdvancedHealthcare

www.YouTube.com/@Dr.SusieWarden3816

www.AdvancedHealth.us

www.LinkedIn.com/in/AdvancedHealth

https://linktr.ee/DrSusieWarden

## How to Get Through Life's S#*! Storm & Start to Posture Up and Take Control of Your Life Checklist

STAY IN YOUR STORM OR TAKE COVER!

Are you in the middle of a "storm of life?"

Are you awake at night worried about the MONEY and energy it will cost to pull you through?

I hear you and have a step-by-step GIFT for you to start to LIVE BETTER and FEEL BETTER.

#postureup

https://linktr.ee/DrSusieWarden

# Dr. Katrina Nguyen

## *From Poverty to Generosity*

*"Stop saying just."* These words rang loud and clear in June 2022, when I attended a four-day boot camp to become the *"best speaker ever."* They still resonate with me to this day.

I have spent much of my life thinking that I am just another refugee who escaped Communist Vietnam and struggled to assimilate into the American culture. I tried to stand out from the crowd during my formative years, by winning school handwriting and spelling contests.

In high school, I was surrounded by classmates whose parents were highly educated, successful, and influential in the community. I longed for a sense of belonging because my parents could neither speak, read nor write fluently in English or even in their own language. They never attended parent-teacher conferences or school open houses. My older siblings always took my parents' places when it involved education. With encouragement from my teachers, I won the highest honor in the school science fair in ninth grade and captured one of four science medallions when I graduated from high school.

I attended the University of California, Irvine, and majored in biology. My love for science was ignited in the seventh grade. However, I did not commit to a career in medicine until my junior year in college. While volunteering in a NICU in Santa Ana, California, I finally put two and two together. A doctor saved my life in a refugee camp in Guam. I wanted to be a doctor to give children second chances.

I faced obstacles when applying to medical school. The Medical College Admission Test (MCAT) seemed like the roadblock to becoming a doctor. During that challenging time in my life, I reflected on my past and realized that I had always learned how to overcome it. What happened next, removed the roadblock. The American University of the Caribbean School of Medicine believed in me and gave me a chance. I graduated from medical school in 2002, and to this day, I continue to make my alma mater proud.

Matt Brauning, a keynote speaker, best-selling author, and corporate trainer, said to me: *"Do me a favor. Stop saying just."* I took those words to heart. That advice changed the way I began to speak about myself. I realized that I wasn't giving myself enough credit. I learned to embrace my accomplishments. I became more intentional about receiving compliments with gratitude rather than humility. Matt made me realize that I was a big deal.

My thoughts of self-affirmation began to sound like this:

- **I am not just a doctor. I am an award-winning, board-certified pediatric gastroenterologist.**
- **I am not just an author. I am an international best-selling author.**
- **I am not just a nonprofit leader. I am the founder of a nonprofit to help reverse the childhood obesity epidemic in America.**

By eliminating the word "just" from my vocabulary, I am learning to limit self-deprecating language. I believe that downplaying my accomplishments is a habit I have unknowingly picked up ever since I began my medical career. I always saw someone who was smarter and more accomplished than I was. As a doctor in my 40s, I still unravel these negative thoughts and habits.

I made it a habit to compare myself to my former self rather than to other people. Was I making progress or staying stagnant in my knowledge and skills? Was I using my time, talent, and treasure to make the greatest impact on the world? Aiming to be better than my former self became my goal each day.

Dr. William Osler, the father of modern medicine and one of the founding professors of Johns Hopkins Hospital, once said, *"A good physician treats the disease; the great physician treats the patient who has the disease."* His sentiments are echoed by Dr. Hunter "Patch" Adams, who the late Robin Williams portrayed in the 1998 film *Patch Adams*. *"You treat a disease; you win, you lose. You treat a person, I guarantee you, you'll win, no matter what the outcome."* Dr. Patch Adams has been an inspiration to me throughout my medical career.

To be a good doctor, one must learn to see the patient as a whole person, not someone with symptoms to alleviate or health problems to treat. It is important to remember the biological, psychological, and social roles in a person's health or disease.

There are certainly acute illnesses that can be cured with medications or surgery. However, there are few chronic diseases for which there is a definitive cure. When medications or surgery is used to treat a chronic disease, patients often trade one disease for another or choose between alleviating certain symptoms while fearing potential side effects. I have found myself often saying this to my patients: *"There is no cure, but there is a treatment for your condition."*

As a refugee who escaped Communist Vietnam at 14 months old, I grew up learning to overcome many barriers to be successful in America. These barriers include knowledge, time, access, finances, environment, motivation, and attitude. I recognized that if I helped people overcome these barriers, I would give them the stepping stones toward achieving a healthier and more affordable lifestyle.

I believe that the best physician is one who can prevent disease development, not solely treat them. A contemporary medical problem, such as childhood obesity, presents an opportunity to prevent chronic disease by empowering people with knowledge, opportunities, and motivation.

In 2014, I formed a nonprofit called Faithful-2-Fitness® to help reverse the childhood obesity epidemic in America. In March 2015, I shared my vision of a childhood obesity intervention program in Rockford, Illinois, that is community-based, stewardship-driven, and can be replicated anywhere in the United States. My impetus for designing a childhood obesity intervention program was this statement from Dr. Adams, *"Our job is improving the quality of life, not just delaying death."*

Before forming Faithful-2-Fitness®, I designed a childhood obesity intervention program in Augusta, Georgia in 2012. The concept was submitted as a grant application to the American Academy of Pediatrics. My pediatric resident and I were awarded a CATCH (Community Access to Child Health) grant. Recipients of a CATCH grant must demonstrate that their proposal can be replicated in any community. Receiving the CATCH grant gave me the confidence to create the program in Rockford, Illinois, and to form Faithful-2-Fitness®.

My journey to forming a nonprofit while continuing to practice medicine was challenging. I'll never forget these words: *"Why would a nonprofit want to help a nonprofit?"* In 2014, after completing a 30-minute PowerPoint presentation, I was met with these words from a gentleman in the audience. He was the CEO of a local branch of the largest nonprofit community service organization in America. These words were followed by dead silence.

In order to form a nonprofit, I had to tackle an inferiority complex. These thoughts were going through my head. I am just another doctor, not anyone featured on TV, radio, podcast, or in the newspaper. I provide care for children who struggle with obesity-related health problems. However, other doctors do that too. Why do I think that I can form a nonprofit to fight childhood obesity? Was I truly an expert on childhood obesity?

I eventually partnered with a local fitness center that asked the right question, *"How can I help you?"* Since 2015, Peak Sports Club has offered a free workout space for one hour every Saturday, along with a volunteer group fitness instructor. After that, the pieces of the puzzle fell into place to make the vision for my childhood obesity intervention program become a reality. People began asking me, *"How can I help you?"* rather than,

*"What's in it for me?"* Volunteers came from different sectors of the community, including dietitians, fitness instructors, nurses, and medical students. Some people came to motivate families during group fitness classes. Our weekly Saturday exercise classes became a source of emotional support for the families.

Community partners who gave time, talent, or treasure to Faithful-2-Fitness® included grocery stores, culinary experts, web designers, attorneys, and small business owners. We offer meal prep classes, farm visits, interactive nutrition lessons, and grocery store tours to teach families that eating healthy doesn't cost more.

We offer at least two 12-week programs per year. I am proud to say that Faithful-2-Fitness® continues to change lives and empower families on their journey to a healthier lifestyle. We give families hope, knowing that they don't need to pay enormous medical bills to learn and implement healthy habits in the home. In addition to our program, we have hosted a 5K event called Fight Obesity Walk with Me every August since 2016. Our event brings together people of all ages, backgrounds, and beliefs, with 150-250 participants annually.

With every challenge, there is always a reward. Over my two decades of practicing medicine, I've observed this to be true: **gratitude breeds generosity, generosity breeds joy, and joy leads to wellness**. Witnessing the positive transformation of the participants in the childhood obesity intervention program over the years and their gratitude for our program is what brings me the greatest joy.

In July 2015, after completing the first program, a mom and her daughter gave me a card that read: The ripple from a single stone cast into the water touches small islands, distant shores… so too, has your teaching. This card reaffirmed that our program helped them overcome a knowledge barrier.

In July 2016, the Rockford Register Star newspaper interviewed a female teenager named Amari. This is what she said. *"I didn't like working out in groups. I wasn't ready for that. But I looked around and saw people going through the same struggles with weight and food. I was thankful I wasn't alone."* She participated in our program from July to October 2015. She reported losing 20 lbs. over one year after completing our program. I had written a letter of recommendation for her, and she was honored as Rockford's Youth of the Year in June 2016 by the Boys and Girls Club for her commitment to leadership and community service. Amari's story reminds us of the importance of emotional support in achieving a healthier lifestyle.

Our program requires the participation of parents with their children. We emphasize that there will be better long-term success in health outcomes, if the family members support each other. We offer scholarships to help families with an initial three-month gym membership after completing a 12-week program. To date, we have offered over ten scholarships to families who have completed at least 80% of their 12-week program.

In October 2019, a teenager named James and his mother received a gym scholarship. Afterwards, the mom sent me this message: *"Dr. Katrina, I just want to say thank you so much for introducing us to F2F. We won't be able to make it to the last two classes because I must now work on Saturdays. But we are in the gym five days a week. James has lost 30 lbs. and I lost 20 lbs. We are thankful for you and the program you offer."* Their story demonstrates the importance of helping families overcome a financial barrier that could help ignite their path to health and wellness. Perhaps this family might continue working out in the gym, or perhaps not. However, getting them into a fitness routine and helping them identify what type of physical activity is immediately achievable is leading them in the right direction.

Sometimes, it's not just about losing weight. We often must step back and look at the bigger picture. Childhood obesity intervention is an opportunity to prevent and even reverse potentially detrimental health outcomes.

In August 2022, two people shared their stories at the 7th annual 5K event. Yvette and Jadon were a mother and son who had been a part of our program for about nine months.

Jadon stepped to the podium and said, *"I have been in Faithful-2-Fitness® for almost a year now, and it has changed my life. I have been diagnosed with diabetes for almost two years now. My A1c before I started the program was 9.9%, and now it is 6.3%. The best part is I no longer need to inject myself with all that insulin as I used to."*

Yvette then shared: *"We have never seen or been in a program where a doctor (Katrina Nguyen) and a dietitian (Christine Gillette), the volunteers, and fitness instructors all exercise with us together as a family—motivating one another and helping us to not focus on a scale but a lifestyle change to better our health to improve our chances of living longer. Thank you for giving your time and treasures and being an inspiration."*

Jadon and Yvette's story reminds us that as a community, we can make a tremendous impact on health problems related to childhood obesity by simply giving families access to fitness activities and being a source of motivation for parents and children to develop a more active lifestyle. Imagine the impact you can make by helping a teenager stop injecting himself with insulin and no longer be diagnosed with type 2 diabetes!

The volunteers who give time and talent benefit from improved physical fitness as a participant in the exercise classes. Local businesses benefit from supporting nonprofits, like Faithful-2-Fitness®, because they are recognized for positively impacting the community.

One thing I've observed is that the culture of medicine has been skewed toward providing sick care, with less emphasis on training clinicians to excel in wellness care. Historically, clinicians are rewarded for the management of chronic diseases, such as those related to obesity, including type 2 diabetes, hypertension, high cholesterol, heart disease, and nonalcoholic fatty liver disease. Clinicians have little incentive to spend time and energy on wellness care and counseling.

I recognize that childhood obesity is a health problem that cannot be effectively managed in an office setting. To be frank, childhood obesity is not an easy topic to address. Obesity is not always viewed as a medical problem by children and parents. Clinicians often hear phrases like *"This is genetic, or This is how I am built. Changing my diet or lifestyle won't make a difference."* Parents and children are uncomfortable talking about their struggles with weight management. When they step into the doctor's office, they are already feeling helpless and hopeless. Children have frequently been bullied at school, struggled with eating disorders, or are undergoing treatment for mental health challenges.

In my experience, in order to have an effective childhood obesity intervention program, it should involve both parents and children. It should be comprehensive, affordable, motivational, and accessible. It should not be focused on watching the scale but on making healthier dietary choices and being more physically active. Families must commit to making changes together in the right direction in order to see a positive outcome in their health.

Prevention of childhood obesity will reduce the financial burdens on the healthcare system in the future. Much of the recent discussions about childhood obesity have been focused on studying the effectiveness of medications or surgeries. As a community, we can reduce the cost of healthcare by incentivizing wellness care. The answer to reversing the childhood obesity epidemic is not more medications and more surgeries. The solution lies in the community lending a helping hand to help families re-learn healthy eating habits and motivate each other to be more physically active.

My journey to overcoming mediocrity can be summarized as this. I am not just another doctor taking care of sick patients. I am a physician who overcame barriers as a refugee and used her lessons to empower people to chart their own path toward health and prosperity.

**Blueprint to Form a Faithful-2-Fitness® Chapter in Your Community.**

The most important principle to follow: The childhood obesity intervention program is supported entirely by the contribution of volunteers of their time, talent, and treasure. Nobody is paid a penny.

**Key Community Partners**

- Registered Agent (attorney) to assist with the establishment of nonprofit status at the state and federal level
- Website/design team
- Fitness Center to offer free gym space for one hour every week
- Fitness Instructors to teach Group Fitness Classes for parents and children
- Dietitian to offer hands-on Nutrition Lessons and Grocery Store tours
- Culinary partners, such as chefs, cooks, and companies that offer meal prep classes
- Grocery stores that offer gift cards to purchase supplies for meal prep classes
- Local Farms for field trips to get education about the source of foods and inspire families to grow their own vegetables.

**Dedication**

I dedicate this chapter to my uncle Phuoc Van Nguyen, who will always be my role model for generosity. He was a bachelor his entire life. His nieces and nephews were his kids. He was an orphan after the Vietnam War, who embraced the opportunity for an education in America. He was a role model for success with his strong work ethic, carrying out his duties faithfully as an employee at Fluor Daniel until his retirement.

He passed away at 63 years old from throat cancer that metastasized to the brain and lungs, even though he had never smoked a cigarette in his entire life. Before he died, he set up an enduring charitable fund called Avocado Trust to support causes related to children, health, faith, and education.

In honor of his life and legacy, I crafted this statement which is engraved on his tombstone. This is how I would like him to be remembered by those who love him and will be known to those who will pass by his gravesite.

**A Lifetime of Simplicity**

**A Legacy of Generosity**

# Dr. Katrina Nguyen

Dr. Katrina Nguyen is an award-winning, board-certified pediatric gastroenterologist, keynote speaker, international best-selling author, and founder of a nonprofit to fight childhood obesity. She is a Clinical Associate Professor at the University of Illinois College of Medicine in Rockford.

She has shared her expertise via EWTN Global Catholic Network, YMCA podcast, and the American Academy of Pediatrics.

She was just 14 months old when her family escaped by boat from Communist Vietnam in April 1975 after the Fall of Saigon. She nearly died twice during her journey to freedom and to live the American Dream.

Dr. Nguyen provides telemedicine services through MyCatholicDoctor and serves as a locum tenens physician. Her Christian faith drives her to serve others. She established a charity fund with Raymond James, and her nonprofit's sponsors include Chick-fil-A and Panera Bread.

She was nominated for the Leonard Tow Humanism in Medicine Award in 2016 and 2017. She was awarded the Faculty and Staff Aureus Award from the University of Illinois College of Medicine in 2017. She was nominated for the Crusader Community Health Annual Spirit of Caring Award, only one of seven nominees in the Rockford region in 2018.

Dr. Nguyen lives in Illinois with her husband, Dr. Marconi Deladisma. She enjoys being a dog mom, gardening, and traveling.

Dr. Katrina Nguyen
Faithful-2-Fitness®
380 Castle Wynd Drive
Loves Park, IL 61111
706-294-7995
mdkatrina1974@gmail.com
www.mdkatrina.com

---

### 3 Steps to a Healthier You

Three tips to jumpstart your journey to a healthier lifestyle.

https://mdkatrina.com/non-profit-leader

# Kathryn D. Regganie
## *Shine Bright*

It was a beautiful, cool February morning. I was still tucked into my bed taking my first deep breaths of the morning and stretching my sleepy body. I was thinking about starting my day with a smile on my face. I then received a phone call from my mother. We had a great conversation, which was strange because she didn't like talking on the phone all that much. It was probably the deepest conversation and connection we've ever had. Although we loved each other very much, we didn't have much of a connection the way that many mothers and daughters do. During that conversation, she said many amazing things that really stuck with me. One of the most impactful things she said was, *"You know, I can see things very differently now. If you could see yourself the way I can see you right now, you would be amazed. Your light shines so brightly. It's just so beautiful."* As I chuckled and visualized the night sky with the stars, some shining brighter than others, Mom said in a stern but loving way, *"And no, this is not because I'm your mother."* I could hear the smile on her face. The interesting thing about this phone call is that my mother had passed away about nine months earlier. This was such a vivid encounter, that it was clearly not a dream. It was a powerful moment with my mother that gave me an important message and a reminder to continue to shine my light, even when it was hard. However, I couldn't see it.

During that time, my husband and I had just moved to another state. I was still struggling with Mom's death. Not only did I have to figure out how to live without a mom, but I also had to build my business up again in a new town with people I didn't know. I was still a bit of a mess. I was not confident that I could build my business and life back to what it had been. In my mind, I knew I could and would do it. However, my heart was still broken.

Because of that phone call, I took some time to sit and reflect on what Mom had said. I could see for myself what she could now see so clearly. Over the next few days, I looked at what I had accomplished and how I'd shown up in the world for myself and for others. I started to see her perspective and realized that I was really good at supporting people to achieve their goals. It was like I was there shining the flashlight or lantern for them, like a guide or facilitator.

Mom's message got me thinking about how to continue to allow myself to shine as brightly as I could in a more conscious way. When I'm not feeling very bright, it comes down to just one simple strategy...

PAY ATTENTION TO ME. It's as simple as 1, 2, 3.

1. Become aware of yourself and how you feel.
2. Decide what you want or need.
3. Clear the clutter/remove obstacles in the way.

**Become Aware of Yourself and How You Feel.**

We are very well-trained to put our focus on things outside of ourselves and to not pay attention to how we are feeling. It's easy to get distracted by social media, TV, work, family obligations, friends, and social obligations. The list goes on and on. Headache, no time for that. Back pain, maybe later. Feeling overwhelmed, isn't everyone? When was the last time you recognized and acted on what your body told you?

I'm really good at supporting people to achieve their goals. However, it is sometimes to my detriment. I can get very wrapped up in the whirlwind of activities that are completely focused outside of myself. As a result, I forget to look in the mirror. I then get tired and grouchy, and my body starts to ache.

When that grouchy feeling starts to creep up, I practice turning inward and focusing on my physical body. I become more aware of myself. I take the time to notice any tension, aches, or pains that I may have. I notice if I'm tired and what my mood is at that moment. When I'm aware of my body, I can go deeper and find ways to regain focus on myself and release those things causing the stress.

What this really means is that I get fully back into my body. It is my navigational system that is very wise and helps me determine what works best for me at each moment. It's about taking time to simply breathe. When I am willing to take up the space in my own body, there is no room for anyone else to take up that space for me.

It is a simple and quick process. I take a deep breath into my feet, notice my feet, and fill them with whatever my feet need at that moment. I then take another breath into my legs and fill them with whatever they need. I then breathe into my torso, arms, neck, and head. I fill those areas with whatever they need as I go along. I sit with that feeling of being full of everything I need at that moment. I feel centered and aligned with my spine. My navigation system is fully functional.

YOU are an intelligent being. There is a part of you that knows what works well for you and what doesn't. If you learn to pay attention to that, life can flow with much more ease and grace.

**Decide What You Want or Need.**

When you come back to yourself and become aware of how you are feeling, the next step is to decide what you want to focus on for yourself. What is most important to you at this moment? What needs to change to make things work better for you right now?

Do you have those people in your life who expect you to be available for them at any time? Being aware of your needs can help create the boundaries you need and create more harmony in potentially stressful situations.

A client of mine had been a bit stressed out because of some family holiday scheduling concerns. She wanted to make sure that she got to see everyone. However, she wanted to spend more time with her mother that year. In previous years, the sister-in-law would call and let my client know when they would be coming. It had worked out fine in past years. However, this year my client wanted something specific. I asked my client what would work best for her, and she gave me the exact schedule. Then I asked if she could let her sister-in-law know what she had just told me about the schedule. Would her sister-in-law be open to it? My client had not even thought to do that before. They thought it was a great idea. She and her sister-in-law got along fine and didn't see any issues with having that discussion. So, later that day, she called her sister-in-law, and they talked about the schedule. Everything worked out well for both parties.

My client had previously just let others take control. She would feel like she should just comply. However, because she had special needs this time, my client took control and let her priorities lead the way. No one got mad or bent out of shape. If you are in the right state of mind, this is really easy to do.

It is very important to be clear on what you need at any moment and create safe boundaries around that. Determine what schedules work best for you and stick with that. Identify the kind of people you enjoy being with and let the others go.

When I started deciding what I wanted, the most important thing I learned was that it is okay to change. Not only is it okay, but you also can't grow and expand without change. Although change is good, it does not always feel good. I learned that when it doesn't feel good, just become aware of what you need to move forward.

**Clear the Clutter/Remove Obstacles in the Way.**

Now that you have decided what you want, you can get rid of those things that don't fit anymore. There may be things you are focusing on that you don't need to focus on anymore. For me, this, of course, includes the cabinets, closets, and dressers. It also included all relationships, even with family.

My first big experience with clearing clutter was when I was going through my divorce. The divorce was very stressful. I was still going to school, my parents needed help, and I also had to keep my head in the game at work. I just could not take on another thing. When I stopped to take a breath, I started to notice the effort I put into relationships and discovered that I was the driver in many of them. I was the one to call to see how they were doing. I was the one to call and say let's go do something. The relationships were very one-sided. I was giving WAY too much without getting anything in return. This was a huge energy drain for me. It had to stop.

I found myself wondering what would happen if I didn't reach out as often or waited for them to call me before I called them again. I discovered that some people didn't notice or didn't care. I have not heard from them since. Some of the people I thought were friends fell off the radar. We just stopped connecting. There was no anger or resentment, just no connection. The people who did care kept in contact. It was much easier. It gave me the space I needed for myself at that time.

I no longer felt that I needed to support people in the same way I had been supporting them. I learned that I had more time for myself by letting go. It felt really good. I felt much lighter and didn't even realize how heavy I had felt in the past. Friends and family who kept in touch with me were much easier to stay connected with because there was an equal exchange of energy. It wasn't always me giving. I was also receiving. It was amazing.

I still practice these three steps. I more easily become aware of myself and my feelings about something. I then decide what I want and clear the clutter that might get in the way. It's a process that can take just a minute or two to accomplish and has a major impact.

Because I practice being aware of myself daily, it has become much easier to be confident in myself and create safe and healthy boundaries with family, friends, and clients. It's easier to say "no" and come up with an agreement that fits better for both sides.

Another big step in this process was when I realized that I didn't have to "fix" things for people. It is not my job to fix things. I am, however, there to support someone on their journey and maybe help shine a light in the direction of their answer.

That phone call from Mom had a deep impact. Her words still linger in my soul after all these years. The message helped me remember that because things change and life gets challenging, we are still very powerful people and have a light to shine in this world. This phone call was Mom's way of reminding me to keep moving forward, shining brightly, so that I could continue to also help others shine brightly.

# Kathryn D. Regganie

Kathryn has a business degree and has been a corporate training professional for over 15 years, teaching and guiding America's top minds into being team players, balanced bodies and minds, and highly efficient creators.

She now focuses on teaching high-achieving women executives how to hold resilience and value even when those dramatic, foundation-shattering moments happen in their personal lives. With her Resilient Woman Leadership program, she makes superwoman impervious to the kryptonite of life. They become more confident, relaxed, effective, creative, and happy in work and life.

Kathryn is known for her honest, grounded, nurturing manner. She is adept at weaving together the mind, body, and spirit to create a unique, safe environment that encourages profound healing.

She is compassionate and intuitive and can connect deeply, so that her clients can feel safe enough to go deeper into their healing process and self-discovery than they thought possible.

Kathryn D. Regganie
Energy Pathways, Inc.
Ridgeway, SC
Kathy@Energy-Pathways.com
www.Energy-Pathways.com

## Which Drama Dragon Sabotages Your Leadership?

The Drama Dragon Quiz will help you learn which Drama Dragon is most likely to sabotage your leadership. Knowing your dragon is important so that you can learn to work better with her and use her for good.

By learning the secrets about your Drama Dragon you can better understand yourself and be the resilient leader that everyone knows you already are.

When I truly identified my unique "Drama Dragon" as I now call it! I found my best ways to tame that dragon, according to the system I've now developed. My confidence started growing with making choices for ME which also showed in my results at work and at home. I felt in control again which allowed for the light my mother reminded me about to shine brightly again.

www.dramadragonquiz.com

# Liz Orvis

## *I Get Knocked Down, But I Get Up Again*

I have never wanted to be mediocre. In fact, when I was younger, my motto used to be, *"I don't go halfway,"* and boy did I live it. When I was in high school, getting a 4.0 GPA was not enough. I felt like a failure if I did not have a 4.5 (bonus points for AP classes). It was not good enough to get a varsity letter in swimming; I had to be a co-captain. I did not celebrate when I made the elite Show Choir, and I was not happy until I was also the president of the choir department. I was in the top 5% of the ACT… across the nation… but I did not get a perfect score. Therefore, I was sure that I had failed.

Nothing that I did was enough. If I got 100%, I wanted 110%. I was making myself miserable. I could never be happy because nothing was ever enough. I tried to overcompensate by being super bubbly and cheering on everyone else. I had many friends (who I never held to the same standards as me). However, inside, I was hurting all the time.

For most of my young life, my favorite population was kids and adults with intellectual disabilities or, as they horrifically called them back in the day, "trainably mentally impaired." I was inspired by all that they accomplished each day. They always faced adversity head-on with a smile on their face. I was very thrilled with each small accomplishment they made… Why couldn't I hold myself to the same standards?

One issue was that many people in my life contributed to the problem. From fifth grade on, I dreamed of being a special education teacher. I could not think of **anything** that I would rather do. I wanted to go to the best college for special education. However, many well-meaning people in my life would tell me, you cannot be a special education teacher! You are smarter than that. Why not be an engineer or a doctor? I kept thinking… don't they need smart special education teachers?

I worked *incredibly* hard in college. I excelled in all my classes. I did extra projects and studies. I learned as much as I could so that I would be an incredible teacher. I volunteered in the Special Olympics State Games (both winter and summer), even though I have absolutely no athletic ability. That was where I learned the amazing motto, *"Let me win, but if I don't win, let me be brave in the attempt."* I had set myself up to be an incredible special education teacher. I could not wait to take on the real world.

**Then Life Hit**

I do not know how much you know about special education teachers. Instead of doing one semester of student teaching, they must do two (one for special education and one for general education). It turned out that while I was a rather good special ed teacher, I was most definitely not a great general ed teacher. I absolutely hated it and could not understand why anyone would teach those students.

I then got into my first special ed job. I was SO excited. There were around twelve students between 18 and 26, with IQs of 30 or less. These were my people! I was going to teach them to communicate, wash their hands, do food prep, do laundry, and so much more! The problem was that the paraprofessionals in my room were significantly older than me and did not share my vision. They considered their job to be "glorified babysitting" and had no intention of teaching anything. I developed all my lessons and materials from scratch. I even bought a laminator and a lifetime supply of Velcro. However, they were not on board and made their opinions known.

**Then the Bottom Dropped Out Beneath Me**

All the trouble that I had been hiding for years came pouring out. I couldn't run away from it anymore. It just caught up with me all at once. I started to go see the nurses every time I had a break, so I could have someone safe to talk to. (Ironically, one of those nurses became my best friend.) They were extremely helpful and supportive. However, I reached the point that I was completely suicidal. They had to take me to the hospital.

I am not sure what you know about inpatient psychiatric stays, but they are awful. You start out in a waiting room, where you often sit for hours. They take you back to a bed with a curtain, where you strip down. They check every inch of your body for marks or injuries. Next, they give you a gown to wear, that never covers your back. You have a "babysitter." It is often at least 12-18 hours before they find you a bed somewhere.

Once you get to where you are staying (which, if you had to take an ambulance, there is a **$20,000** co-pay with my Medicare), they take away any strings/shoelaces and anything with hoods. Your toiletries (if you remember to bring them) are in a separate room, so you have to ask a staff member any time you want to brush your teeth or put on deodorant. Depending on where you are staying, you might be able to choose healthy food options, or it may be slop with thick Kool-Aid that you can chew. I felt like an absolute and complete failure.

### Then it Happened Again… Then Again… Then Again

I lost my job and then another job. This was followed by losing the best volunteer job I had ever had — ten years with the Muscular Dystrophy Association.

I had nothing left. My dream had never been to be mediocre. However, I had somehow surpassed that and ended up at the absolute bottom of the pile!

I kept wondering… Where did I go wrong? Would it have helped if I had an earlier diagnosis? At that point, I had only seen my primary care physician. A study found that more than 80% of primary care primary care physicians misdiagnose Bipolar Disorder, which was my eventual diagnosis. At that time, in the early 2000s, there was a huge stigma about getting therapy or trying medications. Therefore, no one in my life had even considered it. Everyone knew that I was in trouble, but I covered it so well that it just seemed like we needed to just keep fighting. In college, I was always disappointed in myself. I would beat myself with a hammer and give myself bruises all over. However, we just wanted to ignore it.

This was the lowest point in my life. I could not work, and I couldn't take care of myself. I barely had any money (just what came in from SSI and a bridge card). I felt like the ultimate failure. However, it made me eligible to attend Fresh Start Clubhouse, which taught me how to start where I was and build up. I started doing repetitive skills in the kitchen and eventually worked up to creating a website and developing a data program for the Clubhouse!

Through hard work and with a lot of support, I got back to the top! I was able to earn a Master of Education in Applied Behavior Analysis. I became board-certified and was an outstanding Behavior Analyst, helping many kinds of kids on the Autism Spectrum. I thought that I had finally made it out of the depths and was finally going to live up to my potential. Unfortunately, Bipolar Disorder is very much a cyclical disease. While I had good times, I quickly crashed and was no longer able to work.

This was the deepest depression that I had ever been in. It was partly because I felt like I was the ultimate failure. Nothing was working in terms of treatment. We tried every possible combination of medication and every form of therapy. I even did weeks and weeks of electroconvulsive therapy (once called shock therapy) three times a week. It fried my brain, and I lost a good portion of my memory and ability to navigate the world. We finally decided that I needed a residential treatment program. I spent six months at Hopewell Therapeutic Farm in Ohio. It helped me a lot. However, it did not cure me. There really isn't a cure.

When I got back, I felt great. I was sure that I was never going to have any more problems. However, within two months, I was back in the hospital… and then back in the hospital again.

At first, this was incredibly depressing. However, this was when I determined that I needed to have this experience. I had been in incredibly good hospitals with wonderful staff, doctors who consulted with my psychiatrist at home, using a team approach, etc.

Since I now have Medicare Advantage, I no longer qualify for any of these places. I now qualify for "behavioral centers." I was SHOCKED at the difference from what I was accustomed to. The staff was terrible. They obviously weren't being paid enough and were angry all the time. They spent their time watching TV and were very upset if you asked for your toothbrush or to put a load of laundry in the washer. The psychiatrist never met me in person. I met with him over Zoom for only one to two minutes each day. He kept telling me that I was manic, even though I wasn't. As a result, he kept giving me more medication. He asked me what medicines I was on. I started to tell him, and he said: "Not the dosages, I get to pick those!" What?! He also insisted on giving every patient an Abilify shot. I explained to him gently, and then more firmly, that I can't take Abilify because I had a serious reaction to it in the past. It took a LONG time to convince him.

The food was disgusting. It was mostly fried. If there were any vegetables, they were canned and mushy. They had snacks twice a day, which was usually Pop Tarts, Rice Krispies Treats, brownies, chips, etc. The staff would joke about how all the patients gained at least ten pounds during their stay. They even brought the scale into the kitchen and read the patients' before and after weights. This was a HUGE HIPAA violation!

However, an amazing thing happened during that stay. I finally realized that I did not need to have an amazing job to be amazing. I am brilliant, kind, and understanding. I am GREAT with data and mathematics. I am talented at seeing where a person is and developing a task analysis and transition plan to get them to the next step. I have also always been an AMAZING cheerleader!

## That Was When I Started Writing

I discovered that I had the unique ability to put a voice to this population because I am smart, a good writer, and am also living with a serious mental illness. I started a blog and quickly attracted followers. I was making people similar to me... and other people, too... feel heard and encouraged. Maybe I couldn't accomplish all the dreams I had been holding onto. However, maybe I could change the world this way!

Before I started writing this, I spoke to a couple of legislators. I asked them what would be they would need to consider writing a bill that offered better support and conditions for people with serious mental illnesses. They said they first required data. However, that was easy to find. More difficult, however, was the fact that they needed a group of people, especially across the state, to unite around this cause. It was also necessary to find states where similar bills had passed. This was necessary because if they write a bill that does not pass, it can affect their ability to be reelected. However, no state has passed this type of legislation. Some bills have been introduced at the national level. However, none of them have even made it to the house floor for discussion. We need to find someone who is brave enough to try. It will probably fail, but then we will make some changes and try again... and again... and again... until we win the fight!

Over the past forty years, I have learned that overcoming mediocrity does not mean being perfect. It means dealing with the hand that you are dealt. You must ask for help when you need it but continue to fight. It does not mean just surviving. It means thriving! Whatever your situation, you can still have an incredible life. It means setting a goal to make a change in the world and not letting anything or anyone stand in your way!

This is not, in any way, the life that I dreamed of. However, maybe it's better?! I will not stop fighting for people with mental illnesses until they are treated fairly. The treatment must be equivalent to that for people with medical issues. All mental health professionals should be paid at a rate proportionate to their medical cohorts.

I will fight for early diagnoses, less of a disparity in costs, affordable treatment... and eventually a cure. As stated in the Special Olympics motto,

*"Let me win, but if I cannot win, let me be brave in the attempt."*

I may not win, but I will be brave.

How about you?

Will you fight with me?

# Liz Orvis

Liz Orvis is a woman who is determined to change the world. When she was in elementary school, she was on a service squad working with children with Moderate Cognitive Impairments. She loved it so much that she became determined to work in the field when she grew up. When she was 16, she started volunteering with the Muscular Dystrophy Association and was able to see the progress from kids having incredibly short life spans to living full adult lives. This was an amazing experience. She received her bachelor's from Central Michigan University. She became a teacher of kids with Severe Cognitive Impairments, which she loved. Liz eventually earned a master's in Applied Behavior Analysis, became board-certified, and worked as a Behavior Analyst with children on the Autism spectrum. Liz has achieved many of her dreams despite the fact that she has a serious mental illness. Due to Bipolar and OCD, she is no longer able to work full-time. Despite these limitations, she writes a blog and is also working on a memoir with the intention of starting a conversation, supporting people with Serious Mental Illnesses, and making changes in legislation that will benefit people like her. When she was no longer able to work, she lost hope. She had many hospitalizations and even tried Electro Convulsive Therapy (sometimes referred to as shock therapy). When she was at her lowest, she spent six months in a residential program at Hopewell Therapeutic Farm. This was when she discovered the power of writing and the hope that it gave her. She now smiles more often and even has some hope. According to Liz, "If you know someone with a mental illness or suffer from one yourself, please seek help. It's a good world out there. You just have to see it".

Upcoming book: *It's a Hard Knock Life*, coming soon!

Liz Orvis
24225 W 9 Mile Road, Suite 140
Southfield, MI 48033
MentalHealthMomentsAuthor@gmail.com
www.MentalHealthMoments.net
Check out her blog at: www.MentalHealthMoments.net/blog-01
And sign up for updates at: www.MentalHealthMoments.net/Contact-Me

# Tracy Eisenman

## *Get Your Sexy Back*

The issue of belly fat in mature women is centered around two truths and a lie. Belly fat can cause a woman to feel helpless, exhausted, and depressed. It hit me in June of 2022. My youngest son was graduating from university. Since March 2020, I was living in yoga pants and baking bread daily to overcome the blow of losing the twelve exercise classes I taught weekly.

I knew I had gained some weight, but who really cares? It's not like anyone was going to see me anyway. The clothes in my closet had not been touched for years. It had been years since I put on a pair of heels and a dress. I was relieved to see that the graduation was outside and semi-formal, so my highest heels were not in the running. However, my son was giving the commencement speech, and I wanted to represent him in the best way I could. I found a lovely, respectable dress that gathered at the side to hide the muffin top that I now sported. I felt good about myself.

Fast forward to Christmas 2022. My husband showed me a photo of myself and my son on graduation day. Andrew was so handsome in his graduation gown, highly decorated with metals of honor and multiple cords draping across his chest. Then I looked at myself, stunned. I looked like I was seven months pregnant. WHAT HAPPENED TO ME (see the photo on my website)! I flashed back to my father in his later years, overweight, diabetic, lethargic with no energy, and watching TV for the last 25 years of his life. AM I GENETICALLY PREDISPOSED TO LIVE THIS LIFE TOO? This was when I decided it was time to disrupt my lifestyle.

I acquired amazing tools during the COVID years when I studied to become a performance coach. At PCU (Performance Coach University) I discovered how to research my DNA and create an optimal nutrition and exercise plan that would change my body and elevate my mind. For the last 25 years of my life, I wanted to look much different than my beloved father. If not for me, it was for my children and grandchildren.

The journey began. I wanted to lose this belly fat and get my sexy back. Excess belly fat causes women to feel less desirable, unmotivated, and unworthy, not to mention shameful, ugly, and downright out of control. The current solution is to curl up on the couch with a container of ice cream or a bottle of wine and find comfort in a good book with a good story about someone fully engaged in life, the one they wish they had for themselves. When you find the lie and realize the truth, you can begin the process of dissolving belly fat and have a more enjoyable lifestyle now and in your later years.

**The First Truth**

This stage of life is all about the kids and the parents. The children still need guidance and support to make good decisions, and if we are lucky enough to have them around, the parents need care. If they have managed their health in the traditional manner, they will need rides to the doctor's office to pick up prescriptions, and get testing done often. (You still have a chance to change this lifestyle for yourself.)

**The Second Truth**

We are simply guessing at the best nutrition and exercise plan for ourselves. We may read labels, follow a diet prescribed by our doctor who had done minimal testing, or try Keto because our friend did it and it worked for them. We do this because we do not know that there is a better way. The secret to our precise needs is hidden in our DNA. We can now unravel the code and get an exact prescription for our diet and exercise needs. This is a new technology that the scientists and geneticists have dialed in. My chiropractor offers this for $3,000. However, I have found a better way and can bring it to you at a fraction of the cost. You get the same information. Learn more about this at www.getyoursexyback.vip.

**Here Is The Lie...**

If you are a mature woman, you most likely have experienced this. Even men have been taught that this is the truth, and it is simply a lie. I want to believe that people, in general, at their core, want to be good. They want to do what is right. It is a feeling of pride that reaches down to your soul. It starts from our childhood when we are told that good children get rewarded. When our parents praise us for acting "right," we feel accepted and worthy of their love. Is this true for you?

The issue here has been going on for generations. It is the reason that our parents are spending more time at the doctor's office with health issues and are unable to enjoy an active lifestyle in their later years. It is potentially your future if you follow in their footsteps and do nothing to disrupt your lifestyle. The issue is that we have been told that if we are SELFISH, we are wrong. If we put ourselves first, we are bad.

This is a bold-faced LIE. In part, we have misunderstood the meaning of the word due to the level of maturity when it was introduced into our lives. We hear it as a child when we are learning how to share things. For example, a three-year-old wants all the toys in a basket and does not want the sibling to have any. A parent will enter the situation to teach the act of sharing. They say to the three-year-old, you are being selfish. You need to share with your sister. They are punished for taking what they want. Fair enough, but as adults, we turn this word against ourselves. We tell ourselves that if we do something for ourselves, we are being selfish, which has been bad since we were three years old. Not wanting to be bad, we avoid taking actions that appear to be selfish. Many people believe that doing something for themselves is selfish. These things include eating right, exercise, massage, meditation, and many essential healthcare activities that give us a better lifestyle in our later years.

Dispelling the belief that selfishness is bad can lead to less belly fat.

Let us look at the definition of SELFISH. In the American Psychological Association (APA) dictionary, the definition of "selfishness" is listed as: the tendency to act excessively or solely in a manner that benefits oneself, even if others are disadvantaged. If you have ever been on an airplane, you will hear the stewardess say: *"In an event where the cabin loses air pressure, an oxygen mask will fall out of the ceiling overhead. You are to place the mask on yourself first and assist others that need your help after yours is secured."* When you are ready to disrupt your lifestyle, I recommend using your DNA reports to create your nutrition and exercise plan and adding natural fat-burning supplements to speed up the process.

There are many directions to go. Most of them are simply guesses at what is best for you. You can listen to friends, movie stars, and Instagram influencers, or you can unravel the information hidden in your DNA.

# Tracy Eisenman

Tracy Eisenman is the founder of a million-dollar business. She has coached hundreds of women over the last 15 years with her unique style, mixing science and coaching strategies she learned from Jairek and Amanda Robbins. She has worked with American Eagle, The Grateful Dead, and coached Veronique Bourbeau to win Malasysia's 444k ultra-marathon race across the country of Malaysia. She was interviewed with Ted Turner and was featured in Seventeen Magazine.

Tracy empowers women to use their personal DNA code, along with reports disclosing hidden secrets about their health and what may be hiding inside. She implements her boutique program with timely workshops followed by her laser-focused action plans to disrupt your current lifestyle and recreate one that will serve you better for now and your entire life. Her unique style blends high-performance coaching strategies, modern-day science, and the ancient art of martial arts to help her clients create balance and success in all aspects of their lives. Tracy gives her clients permission to dream big and get the results they dream about.

Tracy holds degrees in biology and chemistry, and a certification in performance coaching. She is also a black belt in martial arts and ranked in the top 5 in kumite nationally.

Tracy Eisenman
Tracylinn
68 Skylark Drive
Washington, PA 15301
724-263-0304
TracyEisenman99@gmail.com
www.TracyLinn.com

## Supercharge Your Sexy…
## … and Get Your Sexy Back

Feeling sexy is much more about your beliefs than it is about your current pant size. Recognizing the mental blocks that limit your sex appeal might be the most important step you can take on your journey to getting that fire blazing. Learn to recognize these seven mental blocks.

https://TracyLinn.com/Gift-Sign-Up

# Kathleen Quink Shaw

## *Finding My Way: A Story of Love, Learning, and Determination*

Learning about yourself and figuring out your place in the world is a lifelong journey. Similar to trekking through a mountain range, there are times when you will stumble and fall and lose sight of the path. However, on the flip side, you will crest peaks and experience moments of pure joy and peace that will forever leave their mark on your heart. This could include graduating from college, meeting your first love, or gazing at your newborn's little face for the first time. You will grow and change. That is the beauty of the human experience. We get to explore hundreds of different versions of ourselves. This is the small child discovering the thrill of riding a bicycle without training wheels, the reckless teenager with a wild, rebellious spirit, and the hardworking young adult trying to find her place in the world.

My journey is still a work in progress. However, isn't that the beauty of life, as I mentioned above?

My life began in Quebec, Canada, the country's largest province by area and the second largest by population. Quebec is known for its abundance of maple syrup, its French-speaking locals, and its talented pool of hockey players. Sometimes, I wonder if my very soul was dipped in maple syrup. I am confident in my fun-loving, sweet personality. I suppose I could thank my Canadian roots for that!

When the world was a storm that shook my walls and rattled my windows, my brother, who also needed a family just like me, came along for the ride. We weren't siblings by blood, but siblings by adoption. The world paired us together, and our parents adopted us together from the orphanage we were in. He was 14 months old, and I was only three months old.

My adoptive parents quickly whisked us out of the icy winters of Quebec, moving us to the beautiful nation of Venezuela. Flanked by the tropical islands of the Caribbean and the Andes Mountains to the northwest, Venezuela is a stunning blend of warm turquoise waters and sheer, rugged peaks flecked in forests and tumbling falls.

Despite loving this naturally beautiful land, we didn't stay here long. My adoptive parents relocated us to Ridgefield, Connecticut, and then finally settled in Redding, Connecticut. This is where I spent most of my early life. My school days were spent in Redding.

I knew that I was adopted. From early on, I felt my life was a constant battle of trying to find my place and trying to discover my sense of belonging. Humans need that for their overall well-being. We are a species that thrive off a community and loving interpersonal relationships. This was a missing piece in my life. My adoptive parents didn't quite provide that nurturing environment for me, where I could feel safe enough to explore different paths and people. There were many times when I struggled to let myself be vulnerable enough to make friends. It got lonely! No child deserves to feel like they don't fit in with their community. I struggled to click with the other children my own age. It wasn't because I wasn't kind or funny, I just didn't connect. I have always been on the shy, quiet side. I did have a few very close friends growing up. I turned to the comfort of animals.

When I'm with them, it's like the world's cacophony and chaos becomes a mere din in the background. It is just me and the animals. As I grew older, I determined that I also connected with younger children. Where I lacked nurture in my own life, I wanted to provide that level of affection and care for children and animals.

During my high school years, I had my own horse. She was a mighty, powerful, yet gentle animal with a light coffee brown coat and glimmering, soulful eyes. She and I were nothing short of best friends. Sometimes, the company of a horse or any animal, heals the soul more than any person. Animals are magic in that way. My caring nature for others is the foundation of my journey into early childhood teaching and daycare.

My parents didn't do the best job of parenting. Their silence was like a blade in my heart. They always blamed me when the laundry or house chores didn't get done. I developed a fierce sense of independence and grim determination over time. I rarely rely on others. My childhood taught me that I could only rely on myself. I could either be my own harshest critic, or I could be my own cheerleader. That fiery sense of drive and ambition still propels me to this day.

Once I finished high school, I attended the University of Connecticut. I studied with both grit and passion for four years. I graduated with a BS in Family Studies and a minor in Early Childhood Development. Throughout this part of my life, the core values of caring for and nurturing others carried me through. I knew it was my life's purpose. It was no wonder that I connected so deeply with animals and younger children during those early years. It provided me with the peace that I needed to be able to survive on my own.

After my education, I worked in a couple of early childhood centers. I sure learned a lot about myself, children, families, and what I wanted. It is one thing to learn in college. It is something else to truly live and breathe childcare. I loved watching children's development and the way they learned to grip a paintbrush and hold it steady as they twirled it across the paper, filling it with blue, pink, yellow, and indigo. Children's ability to accept others mesmerized me. Witnessing them make friends, no matter where their peers came from, is inspiring. The years of innocence that I felt were ripped from beneath me.

These lessons and experiences led me to my own adventure. I decided to open my own center. I was now both an early childhood teacher and a businesswoman. I established the center in a perfect spot. Hundreds of children have grown up in this very center for the past 30 years. (Including my three babies!) Many of the first children who enrolled are now teenagers and adults. Some have even sent their own children to my daycare and or have come to work for me. This is a testimony to the success of my daycare center. It has become one of my greatest accomplishments.

However, it is not my only accomplishment. In 1992, I got married for the first time. Young love is often riddled with learning lessons and figuring out what you want out of a relationship. I wound up being married again in 1998. This is where my next greatest accomplishments come in. In this marriage, we had a daughter and a son together. In my third marriage, I had my second son. My children are each a unique blend of the essence of my wild, brave, and caring spirit. They make me smile and laugh. They are the true joys of my life. I am thrilled to say that they still live with me.

I am now a single Mom raising those 3 amazing children! I'm currently in the process of going through another divorce. Ladies should never settle for people or relationships that are no longer healthy for them. As I said, I am a work in progress, still figuring out who I am and my place in the world. We are forever changing with the tides of life.

My world was flipped and was being steered in a strange new direction in 2019. Right before Covid, I found my birth mother. It was a true flurry of emotions. Part of me wondered if I would now have the answers to these questions: Who am I? Where do I fit in? Why was I given up for adoption?

However, fate had a different plan. Life tore her away from me yet again. It was as if the universe didn't want us to cross paths or to get to know one another. However, I am grateful I got to meet her, to learn where I came from, and to catch a glimpse of her life then and now. I learned that I have a younger brother in heaven. I also have a younger sister, who I have adored getting to know.

With that tenacious drive and determination pushing me forward, I am also in the process of developing my online business. I'm not one to rest, as you can see!

This new business focuses on helping parents who might be struggling daily with raising their children. The launch of my online programs will include guides, tools, and ideas for parents of young children.

Many new parents and parents of young children are likely experiencing challenges that they may not have encountered before. There is the classic exhaustion of adapting to a demanding and different sleep schedule, the list of household tasks, and the pressure of providing for your family. Adjusting to the toddler stage can be just as tough as it was when you had a newborn.

My online programs are designed to educate families and parents on the world of early childhood development. Utilizing my decades of experience and education, the programs will help you navigate the bumps and hurdles of your child's foundation years with confidence and joy. Isn't watching our children grow and learn some of life's most precious moments important? As a mother myself, I know this all too well and cherish these memories with my own children.

As a daycare provider for over 30 years, I have seen it all and learned it all. I've cleaned enough pee, poop, and throw-up to last me a lifetime. I have possibly caught every kind of stomach bug in the world. These are some classic side effects of working in childcare. However, my passion and love for childhood development and learning has only grown. I now want to share my knowledge and experience with other parents.

My story is still not over.; There is a lot to look forward to and learn together. I am still trekking through that mountain range as strong and determined as ever, considering the path ahead. There is sunshine and warmth and mountain peaks still waiting for me. It is also amazing to look back now and then and remember how far I have come.

So, would you like to join me? Together, we can foster a caring, supportive community of love, learning, and growth.

# Kathleen Quink Shaw

Being adopted at three months old, Kathleen never felt a sense of belonging. No matter what she did, she never felt good enough for her "parents." It was a feeling that followed her throughout life, a constant reminder that she was the black sheep in her own family.

Despite the challenges Kathleen faced, she learned to be strong. After all, living in a crib for the first three months of your life is no way to start out. As she grew older, she realized that she didn't want any child to feel the way she did — like they didn't belong or weren't good enough. That is when her lightbulb moment struck — she decided to create programs for busy parents to help them navigate the challenges of raising children and to teach them about the importance of strength and resilience. By sharing her own experiences and knowledge, she hopes to make a positive impact on the lives of children and families in her community.

Kathleen Quink Shaw
The Potty Boss
Precious Moments Day Care Center, Inc
8 Edmond Road
Bethel, CT 06801
203-994-4011
tiggy678@yahoo.com
kathy@kathyquinkshaw.com
ThePottyBoss.com
PreciousMomentsDayCare.org

## Potty Training Made Easy

Is Your Child Ready To Potty Train?

- Can your child follow simple directions?
- Does your child show interest in the potty or signal they need to go?
- Does your child stay dry for at least 2 hours?
- Has your child started to hide when they go in their diaper?
- Has your child started pulling at their soiled diaper?

If you said YES to 3 or more of the questions, your child is ready to be potty trained!

Potty Training Made Easy will help you create a routine that works for both you and your child so you can establish a positive relationship with potty training.

https://thepottyboss.com/programs

# Sheri Mills

## *Are You Ready for Your Bucket List?*

I can viscerally remember it like it just happened. It was the summer of 2019. I had a long day at work and was glad to be home. I walked into my living room and reached down to pick up my dog, Tessa, for some quality love time. Suddenly, I was gripped in pain, as if a lightning bolt came down on my body. It was a pain beyond anything I had ever experienced before. The burning sensation shooting down my right arm and the right side of my back was indescribable! I remember asking myself, "What just happened?" I let go of Tessa and immediately grabbed the couch to hold on to something, since I couldn't straighten up right away. I was scared. I was living by myself, and I had no family around to help. That and the fear of not knowing what to do *terrified me*.

It took a while. However, I finally could sit down on the couch but had to lean back into the cushions. I could not lean forward, or the pain would intensify.

I called a friend and told her what I was experiencing. She was not a medical expert, so she didn't have any suggestions for me. However, she said she had a chair I might be comfortable in, so she brought it over. It was a zero-gravity chair, and it became my home for three months. You see, if I even tried to sit upright, or God help me, lean forward, I was in tears with the pain.

**Let Me Give You Some Insight Into My Life Prior to This.**

I was a successful sales executive in the technology field for over 30 years. To succeed, I worked crazy hours and was always networking and on the go. I might have been hitting my numbers and living comfortably; however, I truly didn't have a life. I worked 12-16 hours a day and had weekends to care for the animals and house, which was not a life. On top of that, all of that on-the-go mentality had me not taking care of myself. Yes, I would get the occasional massage and my nails done, but that was pretty much it.

When you are so focused on your career, you tend to overlook your self-care and don't take quality time for yourself. I was always eating on the run, at networking events (which we all know don't have the healthiest foods to eat), eating late at night, and all the wrong foods.

Due to this lifestyle that I had obviously chosen for myself, my body started breaking down. In the past, I was in a couple of car accidents that took a toll on my back and apparently my neck, which had its own set of challenges. This unhealthy lifestyle really set me back. I ended up with arthritis, fibromyalgia, chronic visual migraines, and restless legs syndrome, which kept me up every night. As a result, I absolutely had no energy when I got up. On top of that, I am predisposed to high cholesterol and had IBS (irritable bowel syndrome) at the time. I was a mess, to say the least.

I remember all the times I had to take off to go to doctors, specialists, and imaging center appointments, and finally, I ended up having a few surgeries. All of these did nothing to help.

The medical system in this country needs a lot of work, to say the least. They wanted to do surgeries and pass out medications. This isn't what I needed. I ended up on twelve different medications that were supposed to help ease the pain and control my cholesterol. I felt no different.

I tried acupuncture, lasers, massage, and chiropractic. And the list goes on. I might get a bit of relief for a few days, although at times, it even made it worse. I couldn't win. I thought I was stuck like Chuck and destined to feel pain for the rest of my life.

**I Had a Lightbulb Moment.**

In the beginning of 2021, things were slowly starting to open again after the pandemic. I stopped by a friend of mine's independent pharmacy to catch up. He introduced me to a medical testing device that could read your antioxidant levels and overall health status. I failed miserably and found out that most of the country does as well. I asked why, and he explained that it is all about your diet. There was something about putting my hand on that tester that woke me up. Right there and then, it hit me.

*"NO ONE is going to help you get better.*
*This is something I must commit to*
*doing myself to get back in good health."*

My pharmacy friend introduced me to a health coach, and I started working with her. I learned that my diet was holding me back. Isn't it funny? None of the experts I had been seeing ever spoke to me about lifestyle and dietary habits to stay healthy. No one ever told me there is a way to avoid future illnesses that I may be predisposed to because of my genetics. Crazy, isn't it?

From there, I started my journey of recovery and took back my life. I cleaned out my cupboards and refrigerator of all processed foods, high sugar, high sodium, and anything with ingredients I could not pronounce.

I then started researching farmers' markets in my area. I would make a day of it. I invited a friend or neighbor, which became a time I looked forward to. It was relaxing, motivating, and fun. I started implementing healthy foods, like more fruits and vegetables, into my diet and took away the cheese and bread I loved so much. I researched new recipes that were healthy and how best to cook my new foods for the best absorption. What a difference!

I learned from my journey that a healthy mindset toward food plays a significant role. By committing to planning weekly meals and doing prep for the week, I made time for myself and began to enjoy the cooking process. Knowing what foods to eat at what times of the day was also eye-opening for me.

**Having a Healthy Relationship With Food Can Change Your Life.**

Within just a month, I found that I didn't miss my late-night snacking, all the bread and cheese, fried foods, and even the fast food that was so easy to get when I was on the go. It wasn't fulfilling. It was just food for fuel.

I started making a nice dinner sitting down at the table (instead of the kitchen counter), lighting a candle, and playing smooth jazz in the background several times a week. What a difference this was for me. I found I now savored my meals. I started inviting the neighbors over at least once a week for a new dish I discovered.

You know what? In a very short time, I did not miss any of the foods that I used to eat. This doesn't mean that I haven't had a cheat moment occasionally. That is OK. I found that when I went out for my favorite fish and chips after being on my new nutritional plan, my body told me never to do that again! I felt awful.

It is amazing how our bodies adjust to what we feed it. Years ago, I was going to journal my meals since my gastroenterologist had told me to stay away from onions and garlic for my IBS. I told him that they were my main staples when cooking, etc.... I never stuck with the journalling. If I had, I may have realized sooner how my diet was really affecting my health. (Don't worry; onions and garlic are not the culprits for me, but I did find others that were.)

We all have different bodies and different reactions to foods, so there isn't one diet or meal plan that fits all. Once I learned this and was successful in making changes to my own lifestyle, my health improved greatly. My cholesterol is lower than it has ever been, there were no more migraines, the inflammation is completely gone, and I no longer live in pain. My IBS is under control. I now sleep like a baby (no restless legs) and wake up with a renewed vitality to take on my day. I am a new person! A huge bonus for me was, without even trying or thinking I wanted to lose weight, 38 pounds fell off me in three months and has not returned. I had tried for over 20 years to lose weight with absolutely no success.

**This Transformation Inspired Me to Go Back to School and Become a Functional Nutrition Coach.**

It has allowed me to help others obtain a healthy relationship with food and get their health back. This has become my passion. If I can make changes at 60, I know I can help others obtain the same level of success.

Getting back to 2019, I saw no way out of that life of pain. I felt like I just had to push through and get by. I couldn't enjoy the simple pleasures of life. I really enjoyed gardening, dancing, and walking on the beach. All of these were off-limits to me since I couldn't get through it. It was a struggle. I knew that my future of traveling and doing all the things that I had on my bucket list of wants and desires was never going to happen. My bucket list is now growing because I no longer have a fear of getting out there and participating in life. What a wonderful feeling!

If any of this resonates with you, I feel your struggle. You can flip the script of your destiny and bring back the health you desire to go after your bucket list of adventures. What are you waiting for?

**Sheri Mills**

Sheri Mills is a heart-centered Functional Nutrition and Health Coach, entrepreneur, and speaker. She is the CEO and Founder of Your Wellness Redefined Inc. and the Co-founder of Functional Wellness Network.

Living with constant pain and her own health issues for over 27 years, Sheri discovered, with the help of a Health Coach, that through nutritional and lifestyle changes, along with amazing supplements, she is now living pain-free!

This led her to go back to Functional Medicine school and give back through her knowledge to help others live a better quality of life. Sheri offers personalized programs for each client and guides them while they implement life changes so they, too, can achieve the results they need to live their best life naturally and full of renewed purpose, joy, and vitality.

Sheri Mills
Your Wellness Redefined
Pompano Beach, FL
945-899-8488
Sheri@YourWellnessRedefined.com
https://YourWellnessRedefined.com

## **Release Inflammation Through Proper Nutrition**

Chronic inflammation, prevalent among us, paves the way for numerous diseases and health conditions.

This guide presents a strategy to eliminate foods promoting inflammation and integrate healthy foods that may regulate such effects. You will find beneficial recipes, enabling progress toward your health objectives.

https://antiinflammatoryguide.now.site/home

# Georgiana Danet

## *From Eating Rotten Tomatoes to Being a Successful International Coach*

I was living in a dictatorship in Romania, under very harsh conditions. There wasn't much food and we only had electricity for two hours per day. The heating was run by electricity. Therefore, in the wintertime, the temperature in our flat was minus 10 degrees Celsius (14 F). We had food coupons, which allowed each person to receive a limited amount of food per month. I come from a modest blue-collar family. My parents did their best under the circumstances. That was life during my childhood and teenage years. It made me ask myself a lot of existential questions about human nature, God, justice, and human rights.

Then, in 1989, the dictator was executed. I was in my last year of high school. I decided to study at university, the first ever in my family. In that year, it was possible to attend two university education programs at the same time. I chose journalism and foreign languages. I also got a master's degree in journalism. I saw a poster in the city about yoga classes that were starting soon. During Ceausescu, everything related to spirituality was forbidden. Therefore, being able to go to yoga was really a treat, considering the past conditions.

I went to meet the yoga teacher and asked her:

*"Can I change my destiny to the better with yoga?*

*Yes, you definitely can!"*

I joined her yoga class. I have been practicing yoga and learning a new technique/aspect every week since then.

My parents were earning an honest (poor) living. Therefore, my monthly allowance did not always cover my expenses. I took jobs while studying whenever I could. However, I sometimes had to manage without. This meant that sometimes I made myself a salad out of rotten tomatoes (whatever I could scrap off them) and rock-hard bread (that I broke with a hammer so I could bite it without breaking my teeth). For a month, I ate boiled rice one day and cornbread on another, etc.

I was determined to create a better life for myself and my family.

While still in university, I thought to myself:

*"I will write a book about esoteric karmic astrology, and all the income from that book will go to my parents."*

I was researching and studying for it all of the free time that I had. I then wrote it in two weeks. That was my first book. I was very happy that I now had the freedom to write about spiritual topics without risking ending up in jail or "disappearing," as happened many times during the communist regime. However, it didn't bring the great income I was hoping for, to be able to support both my parents and myself.

**The Law of Attraction**

As soon as I finished my master's thesis, I started searching for a job. Nothing was fitting my "savior" plans. Therefore, I decided to use one of the yoga techniques I teach to materialize/to attract the job I want. I started applying the method daily for a couple of hours. This involved clearly visualizing the type of work I do and the amount on my paycheck at the end of the month. After six weeks, I got the visualized job, with a paycheck three times more than what both my parents were earning per month. I was having a perfect blend of work and spiritual life — the "materialized" job and the inner spiritual life on the yoga path, practicing four to six hours daily. However, there was still room for improvement.

My soul was signaling to me that (my) life had more to offer.

**The Great Move**

When I was 26, I decided to move to Sweden. Three weeks later, after putting my things in order in my home country, I left for Sweden.

I knew only one person there. I did not speak the language. I had very little money. I had two suitcases with me: one with all my yoga materials and one with some clothes.

To quickly learn Swedish, I started studying it by myself. Then, I applied to a local university in the city where I was living. Just that year, there was an opportunity to study two faculty programs simultaneously. Therefore, I studied sociology and computer and work science. It was quite a struggle in the beginning. I could read Swedish. However, it was not so easy to understand the spoken language. For a while, listening to Swedish or Chinese was all the same to me. Therefore, I asked my teachers to give me the lessons in advance. This allowed me to read them to better understand what was being said during the classes. They were kind enough to help me. In this manner, I learned Swedish in one year.

After graduation, I also got a master's degree in sociology and work science and invented a research method.

While studying, I was also teaching yoga and self-development. Soon after, people started inviting me to give self-development weekend workshops in different countries. In less than seven years, I was touring with workshops in 15 countries, and in over 50 cities.

Many of them were asking me:

*"Can I read what you teach in a book?"*

At that moment, I only had published one book about esoteric, karmic astrology.

I said to myself:

*"If they request this, it means that I will have to write more books. I wrote my second book in three weeks, writing 10-14 hours per day. The third book took four months, while maintaining a daytime job and running a mystery school every evening, with four branches in four different cities."*

I could now answer:

*"Yes, you can read about what I teach in the two books that I have published."*

## Going Global in The Digital Era

After 20 years of living in Sweden, running yoga and self-development classes every evening, a student of mine asked:

*"But Georgiana, why don't you create some of your brilliant workshops as evergreen online courses, so the valuable information you offer can reach much more people?"*

As a result, the next epic journey started. I worked hard for many months, writing, creating videos, designing a webpage, and learning everything that was to learn about running an online business with evergreen courses. People from different countries soon wanted to have one-on-one coaching sessions with me. They wanted to learn how to eliminate stress, develop themselves from a spiritual point of view, and trigger an inner alchemy process to fulfill their needs to be healthy, stress-free, harmonious, and evolved human beings who regain their innate superpowers.

I had to answer this question for myself:

*"What makes working with me unique?"*

There are millions of web pages with coaches offering similar services. I had to distill 33 years of my practical experience and offer people the pure essence of spiritual knowledge and science. It was necessary to offer true self-development, that was simple to understand and easy to apply, tailored to every individual's uniqueness.

It took me months to do this "distillation" of all my experience. At the end of this effort, I created the C.U.R.E. PROCESS:

**C**ause Identification

**U**nderstand

**R**emove

**E**mpower

My clients receive spiritual knowledge that is put into action, with clear methods to apply in everyday life! The feedback I receive from them is amazing! For example, when Susan contacted me, she was already in a very stressful situation in her life. Since she was a high achiever, she wanted to do it "all right." However, it didn't help. The reverse was true. Her boyfriend ended their relationship, and things were too stressful at work. Everything took its toll. Susan couldn't cope with it anymore. As a result, she ended up being hospitalized due to burnout and stress-related psychiatric illness.

As soon as she left the hospital, we started the C.U.R.E. process. After six weeks, she managed to eliminate the root cause of her stress and mastered her energy to such a degree, that she found her true love and a much better job. Soon after, she got married and started a family. Susan told me that since she was both physically and mentally exhausted, she was lying on the floor in her bathroom in despair. She went all the way to waking up every morning enthusiastic about the new day ahead, well-rested, and supercharged.

In connection with going global, I was invited to be a co-author of two books:

*Unzenable* – a guide to stress less and be more.

*Beyond the Pose* – a short book on the science and art of yoga.

## Corollary

Looking back at my life, I feel humbled and very grateful. If someone had told the 18-year-old me that I would be a successful international coach and author, I would have told them to get a reality check and invited them to my rotten tomato salad.

Having this life experience, I can hardly wait for the next epic adventure!

# Georgiana Danet

Georgiana teaches self-development, holistic yoga, inner alchemy, and stress elimination. She believes that every one of us has an infinite potential just waiting to be awakened and used up to 100%. With this online hub, her goal is to assist in the awakening of your true potential and to serve you. Therefore, she can fulfill your needs to be a healthy, stress-free, harmonious, and evolved human being who can regain your innate superpowers.

What makes working with her unique?

- You receive true self-development that is simple to understand and easy to apply. It can then be tailored to your uniqueness.
- You get access to the C.U.R.E. PROCESS = Cause Identification, Understand, Remove, and Empower.

- We start together where you are now. This may be a bit stressed and disconnected from your true core. You can go all the way to being healthy, relaxed, de-stressed, powerful, and balanced. You receive spiritual knowledge that is put into action, with clear methods to apply in everyday life!

The end results:

- Awakening of your true potential
- Feeling healthy, relaxed, de-stressed, and full of energy
- Evolving and developing the SELF
- Radiating confidence, strength, and harmony
- Clarity and Enlightenment
- Feeling at peace and empowered
- Serenity and unshakeable tranquility
- Thriving in the career department, without the need to slow down
- Work-life balance and satisfaction
- Integrating career and self-development in a harmonious way
- Bringing spiritual perspective and tools to your life and your business

Holistic Life Hub™ is an online mystery school for high-achieving women. It distills 33 years of practical experience and offers you the pure essence of spiritual knowledge and science. With a focus on a unique combination of neuroscience, psychology, and spirituality, Holistic Life Hub™ offers precise self-development that's simple to understand and easy to apply.

Georgiana Danet
Holistic Life Hub™
Järnvägstorget 15 B
Karlskrona 37132 Sweden
Evolve@HolisticLifeHub.com
https://HolisticLifeHub.com

## Serene Living — Free Webinar

Breathe deeply! Relax! Go within your source of inner peace with easy steps to follow. Serene living is possible here and now for you!

https://holisticlifehub.thinkific.com/courses/serene-living

# Barb Gabaldon

## *Storms of Adversity:*
## *The Quest for Breakthrough*

Have you ever thought that life would go one direction, only to find yourself thrown into storms of adversity going the opposite? I am pretty certain many of us can answer a resounding, yes! These storms affect our careers, marriage, family, health, finances and more, stealing our dreams, confidence, and joy. I have experienced many epic storms, some more tragic than others. Throughout my quest for a breakthrough, I work to consciously embrace that it's not what happens to us that really matters, but what happens in us as a result. That, my friend, is a choice! To accept this powerful truth brings us to realize that, regardless of circumstances, we all have a measure of personal responsibility, even if the circumstances were completely beyond our control. In sharing a portion of my story, I hope to fuel your quest to authentically use life's storms to break through to your truest dreams and goals, and along the way, uncover a deeper sense of gratitude, grace, and purpose. It is this empowering hope and your quest to take action to victoriously overcome that will bring you through the storms of adversity to reach your highest destiny.

In the fall of 2007, I stepped back onto American soil after nearly three months and nine countries exhausted from traveling 36 hours from Tanzania. I had no clue how drastically life was about to change. Days before leaving on this ministry and humanitarian tour, I placed my life savings in what was to be a well-secured, legally backed by four governments, 90-day investment to fund the final expenditures of a multinational case bringing someone of high stature to justice. The well-connected American leading the case was closely vetted and believed to be above reproach. Suffice it to say, that was not the case. An investigative reporter discovered a cover-up to keep other well-known individuals and agencies from embarrassment. After working for four years trying to retrieve my funds, I never saw a single cent. I was left to rebuild with nothing more than sheer determination and a level of gratitude I had yet to discover.

Wait. What? "Gratitude?" Yes, gratitude! I say that because I had just spent weeks traveling to African cities, jungles, and villages. I had witnessed poverty on a level far beyond the American T.V. screen; eight-year-old children in dilapidated boxes on the side of dirt roads doing their best to survive and *raise* younger siblings alone. Street kids sniffing the leftover cans of paint, not for the high, but for its ability to ward off the pains of starvation. The only drops of water scooped up for human consumption came from filthy ravines where animals defecated. I could go on. My point is that I had no place for woe is me after witnessing such a travesty. I was back in my home country drinking clean water, eating food from fully stocked stores, and being taken in to stay in a manicured suburbia home. I remember standing in Starbucks with a friend, anxious to hear about my travels. The chatter of strangers nearby troubled my soul as inconsequential complaining poured faster than designer coffees flowed. I wanted to scream, *"Seriously? What are you complaining about? Your ten dollars will feed a starving widow and her children rice and beans for a month!"* I remained silent. However, I came face to face with a personal decision; regardless of my circumstances, I would do my best to maintain an attitude of gratitude. I admit that many times, it was easier said than done.

Simultaneously, while settling back into American life, the chatter of the Global Financial Crisis was growing. People began losing homes and jobs at a record pace. Some just walked away because they felt too far underwater to stay in their homes. Perhaps you were caught in this crisis and suffered from corporate lending practices, losing retirement accounts, businesses, and more? Many more have experienced tremendous loss from the more recent pandemic and lockdown. Sadly, hundreds of thousands of lives were lost. Many were left with long-haul health challenges. I faced extreme trauma as my daughter, who was in her early forties with no pre-existing conditions, lay in ICU on a ventilator and ECMO heart-lung bypass machine, fighting for her life for 55 days from this horrific virus. I again had a choice to make. I could cave in under the imminent fear of losing her, or I could stand strong in my faith, reach deep inside, and find gratitude for the measure of last-ditch medical efforts she was receiving. I chose the latter, doing my best to stay strong for her, my grandchildren, and all those who love her. Many from around the globe stood with us in prayer, believing for her miracle. Praise God she survived and miraculously came home to continue healing, re-learning to walk, talk, feed, and shower herself!

I heard chatter again. Some adamantly believed the pandemic was a hoax or worse. Days after my daughter came home, I was plagued with the same debilitating virus, and again eight months later. Remarkably, I was never fully admitted to the hospital, but definitely had to fight for my life! My first round was several weeks before I was strong enough to sit up and be showered. It took me three days to eat one banana. I really wasn't sure I'd see my birthday later that month. My daughter and I are eternally grateful to be alive, despite being long haulers with continued challenges. Both in 2008 and again in 2021, life, as we had once known, was forever changed. Choosing to keep the faith and believe in miracles, paved the way for gratitude and grace to prevail; thanking God for life, well before healing manifested itself in the midst of a raging storm. We have since lost my 22 year old grandson.

Soon after returning to the U.S. in 2007, I was invited by a group of U.S. developers to serve as a liaison for a sizable nine-figure development project in the South Pacific. My interpretation was that I'd get paid to keep big egos in check and negotiations going smoothly through to contract signing. Though still without a stable income and staying on with friends while working on the return of my funds, I agreed to the extremely generous opportunity from these developers, knowing I'd be more than well-compensated upon the project's final signing. I saw it as a way to not only financially stabilize myself and help my family, but also to aid my desire to bring clean drinking water and educational and nutritional opportunities to help stave off childhood slavery throughout Africa. I worked tirelessly day and night across five time zones for ten months to keep this proposed development on track.

In late September, almost one year after my return to America, I arrived at the Hyatt Regency in San Diego to greet the international dignitaries, investors, and project developers for their final signatures on the deal. As usual, I was the only woman at the table. The penthouse view overlooking the renowned San Diego skyline and the Pacific Ocean was magnificent. What was unusual is that it was the same day the Great Recession's bailout legislation in answer to the global financial crisis failed by thirteen votes in the House of Representatives. We would all be informed of this by the lead project developer's aide quietly sitting nearby with a headset on watching several news screens. He leaned over and whispered something in the developer's ear, who then announced the shocking news to the rest of us at the table, contract, and pens in hand, with only one signature remaining to finalize the deal. Instead, the two international dignitaries pushed their chairs back and informed us they were forced to decline the project based on America's government's unwillingness to stand and clean up its economic mess. The room was silent. There was nothing to say, and everyone knew it. We soon dispersed, and limousines arrived to whisk the dignitaries up to Los Angeles and the project developer and his aide back to their private jet. After farewells, I returned to the hotel disappointed and exhausted. I sat on a bench just off the lobby and did my best to hold back a flood of tears. A few days later, legislation did pass, but it proved too little too late to save the project. I had worked non-stop for ten months and would make my way back to Northern California defeated with less in hand than I had when I began. There would be no final contract signing. There would be no financial compensation for my effort.

Perhaps you have felt defeated after months or years of effort. What do we do when life throws insurmountable speeding curve balls at us? How do we go from tragedy to triumph, when we find ourselves sucker punched and sometimes even circling back again? What do we have control over? Maybe you're facing a pressing health challenge, the loss of a loved one or relationship, or pressing issues with your children. Maybe it's an unsatisfying job, business, or financial crisis putting your victory at risk. We do have a choice. It doesn't always feel like that at the moment, but we do have a choice! We can cave, or we can rise... this is what we have control over! That is all we have control over in any situation.

What does overcoming look and feel like throughout the journey? This and many more discoveries were made over the ensuing months and years. There are lessons and strategies that I long to share and support you to overcome adversities and recalibrate your mindset. They will help you to dream again, to reach deep and once again recall lifelong goals, and to discover all is not lost. Lessons are there, growth awaits, and the future is brightly at hand, despite darkness attempting to camp out. It all begins by taking a step back, giving yourself permission to feel your truest feelings, walking through forgiveness, and reconnecting with your authentic self to usher back your deepest desires you may have long buried and forgotten. You must reach out for genuine support, so your breakthrough provides space to move you towards success. Skipping over any of these or other important steps will only keep you from reaching the fullness of your destiny and the genuine happiness you deserve.

Here's part of what my plan looked like following the loss of the international project. I was desperate and sent out resumes for months with no response. As discouragement and fear tried taking root, I dug deep down inside to unbury my childhood dream of attending college. Now in my early fifties and with a bleak financial situation, this thought sounded ludicrous. However, I decided that I had four months to obtain gainful employment, or I would attend college if a position didn't present itself. I sent out at least a hundred resumes for every level of job out there. I had one phone interview and no offer. I became a full-time college student on a traditional 25,000-student college campus that fall. I went on to complete three associate degrees with honors, develop a World Impact Club, serve on the student council, and become a lifetime member of Phi Theta Kappa Honor Society, the largest honor society in the world; where with fellow society members, we earned a top 20 international award out of 1200+ colleges for an inner city elementary school mentorship project I directed. I was blessed with seven scholarships, receiving several six-figure offers to transfer to colleges across the country. I declined them to stay close to my grandchildren and was offered a paid internship at one of the country's top public relations firms by a Board of Trustees of my local college. My "ludicrous" plan was to simply try my best to get through classes in obscurity with the end goal of earning a Master of Arts (MA) degree. Instead, I also had three submissions published in a literary journal and was voted by my much younger peers, our professors, and administrators to deliver the commencement speech at our graduation, attended by some 4,000 guests, including my late father. What an honor! I shared the power of gratitude, citing the story of a single pen based on my journey throughout Africa, and confessed I hadn't walked a graduation stage since the 8th grade. That's right, the commencement speaker hadn't graduated from high school.

Now armed with an undergraduate degree finished summa cum laude, my dream to earn a Master's degree is just one last course away, and my childhood dream is coming to fruition. I have overcome countless other circumstances with family, finances, and health, some extremely tragic. However, now in my 60s, I am proof that it is never too late to keep persevering, to keep learning, and to continue reaching towards our breakthroughs and achieving goals. We will fall and will get back up again and again. We will continue cultivating gratitude and grace to make a difference in our own lives, in the lives of those we love, and in the world around us. We do have a choice!

Throughout this journey, I've learned forgiveness, gratitude, and perseverance on a whole new level. I often half-joke that I've earned a PhT degree… that's a doctorate degree in "Persevering Hard Times." I've caught so many curve balls, dropped some, overthrown some, and learned to pivot and keep running bases, even when it meant barely crawling. I have kept my faith in God, fertilizing grace and gratitude with an overcoming mindset, even in the worst of tragedies. I remain focused on my quest to reach more breakthroughs and achieve more goals serving family, community, and the world around me. I am determined to continue giving my best to navigate life's many challenges with the strength of faith, gratitude, and grace paving the way!

I have presented overcoming principles with diverse audiences from at least 50 different countries throughout the United States, Europe, and Africa. They have included everyone from global dignitaries and professionals to those in shelters, refugee camps, and behind prison walls. Storms affect us all, and the principles to overcome them are non-discriminating. It is my honor to support you in overcoming storms of adversity, embracing breakthroughs, and reaching for your highest dreams and goals, no matter what your age or where you find yourself. A truly epic life is inside you, waiting to be unleashed, and you are the deciding factor! Together, we can break through one step of grace and gratitude at a time.

For coaching, speaking, retreat, and webinar information, please visit: www.BarbGabaldon.com

**Dedicated in Loving Memory**

My Father and #1 Cheerleader, James R. Simmons (1935 - 2018)

My Precious and Talented Grandson, Jordan W.L. Drummer (1999 - 2022)

# Barb Gabaldon

Barb Gabaldon is an international author, speaker, coach, mentor, and humanitarian. She has a strong love for God and holds a Master of Arts degree in Organizational Management from the University of Arizona and undergraduate degrees in Communications, English Literature, and Arts and Cultures. For decades, she is often the only woman repeatedly offered a seat at the table in corporate boardrooms.

Barb is an International Evangelist and Humanitarian Advocate, especially speaking for those most vulnerable. She shares the love of Jesus, empowering and equipping others for His service. She has trained and mentored diverse personal, professional, community, and faith-based audiences, both one-on-one and among thousands. She has presented to world dignitaries from over 30 countries, spoken hope to those in refugee camps, and redemption in maximum security male prisons. She also speaks at leadership conferences and to various retreat audiences of all ages and backgrounds. Barb visits schools, orphanages, and hospitals and has a heart for today's youth. Along her own path of personal tragedies and breakthroughs of triumph, she has garnered tremendous insight and deepened her compassion for others.

Her determination and strong faith allow her to continue overcoming incredible challenges. Whether it's her health, finances, family, or tragic loss, she continues to persevere and break through to achieve astounding victories. She is well respected for her willingness to be generously transparent in sharing insightful lessons and genuine encouragement.

Barb resides in California with her rescued Siberian husky, Sky, and has two adult children with families of their own. She is passionate about her role as "Nana" to six grand and two great-grandchildren, with some "bonus" grands added along the way. In 2022, her family lost her twenty-two-year-old grandson, Jordan, a talented artist and natural-born athlete. In her spare time, she cultivates succulents and houseplants, enjoys painting, mixed-media art, and designing residential interiors and landscapes.

Barb Gabaldon, M.A.
California, USA
Info@BarbGabaldon.com
www.BarbGabaldon.com

## The Quest for Breakthrough

Take a moment to ask yourself five questions to help you prepare yourself for a breakthough. You can apply this to your personal and professional life.

http://barbgabaldon.com/gift-page/

# Patricia Marie Larsen

## *The Many Triumphs of Recovery and Healing*

Recovery is about so much more than just drugs and alcohol. In my case, recovery and healing involved a whirlwind of issues.

First, there was the recovery from a loving but, at times, dysfunctional upbringing, which many can relate to. My healing began with the acceptance and forgiveness of my family's imperfections, which involved a variety of complex issues. I also had a father who struggled with substance abuse and passed away at the young age of 47. This was the beginning of a permanent change in my life. I learned very quickly to try my hardest to live in the moment and prioritize the relationships that I valued the most. Although my father was one of my biggest supporters, in his later years, substance abuse interfered with his marriage, profession, health, and personal goals. This, in turn, affected the security of our family.

As the years went on and I ventured into adulthood, I seemed to gravitate more toward people who had a similar background to mine — some who also came from experiencing some trauma and dysfunction in their households.

In my earlier years, I also had experiences with alcohol and other substances. Due to the situations and outcomes that I experienced throughout my life, I was able to put my use of any mind-altering substance behind me quickly without a formal program. I believe that I was literally "scared straight." From what I could see, the use of a substance in myself and those I knew seemed to add more chaos to my/their lives than peace. Early in my twenties, my observations eventually led me to total abstinence from mind-altering substances.

More healing began after I had my second child and purchased my first home. This was about six years into my marriage. At this point in my life, I was in my late twenties and had much to prove to myself and to the world. Due to my change in lifestyle and my abstinence from tobacco, alcohol, and drugs, I was more energetic than ever and had the desire to live a healthier lifestyle. I was in top physical condition at this time, striving for perfection in all areas. My home, surroundings, health, and spirituality began to heighten. I became more involved in my local church through a close friend and a baptismal visit for my youngest daughter. From there, for several years, I was involved in adult faith-sharing groups that introduced me to other life perspectives.

As time passed, I began to realize that my spouse and many others in my circle had struggled with alcohol and substance abuse. The more I was around it, the more I realized its indirect negative effect on my life, even though I was not using myself.

I began to often hear the term adult children of alcoholics on television, in conversation, etc. It was by chance, at the peak of my thoughts, that a six-week course was offered through the county to raise awareness about the subject of adult children of alcoholics.

**Finding a Relatable Support Group and Becoming Accountable for Your Own Actions Is Essential to Begin the Healing Process.**

I was naturally very interested and attended. This class took my healing to a different level. I could identify with much of the material and now had validation and education that specifically related to me and this topic. It was a true eye-opener and bolstered my curiosity to learn more.

Over the years, I watched many people deteriorate from alcohol and drugs. It was mind-boggling to me. In my way of logical thinking at the time, I would say to myself, *"What is the problem?" "Why can't they just quit?" "Why would someone want to lose everything?"* even their lives. It was beyond my understanding at the time. I thought that a simple intervention and good conversation would do the trick and put that person back on track. This was an extremely naive way of thinking. I eventually realized that addiction is a disease. It's just not that simple.

**Educate Yourself About Addiction Formally or Informally.**

When I was in my late twenties or early thirties, I began taking general classes at the local community college. My first class was psychology class. I have always had an interest in what makes a person tick. I found this class to be extremely interesting and was looking forward to continuing my formal education. Having a love for short informational reads, I ran across a pamphlet pertaining to the track for addiction counseling available on campus. I can remember feeling very excited that I found a career that was attainable in a fairly short time frame and on a subject that I could identify with. From there, it was history, although it took me a bit longer than the norm to get through the program due to work, family, and home responsibilities. I was eventually able to graduate and become licensed. My educational journey was just enough for me to learn how important a balanced lifestyle truly is. Along the way, I grew in many ways, gaining an education, self-confidence, and true insight into a subject that has always been dear to my heart.

Fortunately, every individual can find the opportunity to be supported down the path of recovery. The challenge is to discover and utilize the resources that are available and suitable for them. With every experience, the hope is to gain more knowledge and insight, learn new ways, and in general, learn to cope on a one-day-at-a-time basis.

Later in my forties, when I completed my internship and began working as an addiction counselor, I felt inadequate at times. I thought to myself, *"Do I truly have the capabilities to help others?"* After all, I was still growing and healing myself. That feeling did not last forever. Seeing others start their journey and begin to heal was yet another miraculous experience. It showed me that there is never a time when giving up is an option. Seeing the growth and change in others gave hope to all involved in the process. Knowing that change can occur and will occur if a person is willing is very encouraging. We all take a few steps forward and, yes, a few steps backward at times. However, the key is to never give up on yourself.

**Continue to Heal by Caring for Yourself Physically, Intellectually, Emotionally, and Spiritually in the Hope of Creating a Balanced, Peaceful Existence.**

Today, at sixty, I am currently working on a more personal level with individuals. I can truly say that my years working at the treatment center renewed my faith in humanity and heightened my sense of what life can offer. Through my journey, I began to connect to individuals on another level and was able to grow and learn more than I ever could imagine. What I experienced through getting to know the women was beyond powerful. I knew that abstinence from substance abuse is only a small part of the healing process. Most of us are continuously working on overcoming obstacles, trying to better ourselves, and searching to attain inner peace and contentment.

I am no longer striving for perfection and am definitely not in my best physical condition. However, I have been able to attain a level of inner peace and contentment and a love for life, along with all it has to offer. This journey of recovery and healing is not easy. It goes on for a lifetime. However, it is well worth the effort. I often would hear individuals say, *"Every day is a gift."* I must say I have never heard a truer statement.

Prioritizing what is important to you is often difficult. However, it is truly important to identify this to serve yourself well. Self-assessment can help identify this and allow you to work toward goals that eventually lead to a most fulfilling life and a more peaceful existence.

This opportunity to tell my story is dedicated to my children, grandchildren, and all the women and families struggling with substance abuse. It is in the hope that they, too, will find the strength to attain a satisfying level of inner peace and contentment.

# Patricia Marie Larsen

Patricia Larsen is 61 years old. She has been married for 44 years — since high school graduation at 18 in 1979. Her first daughter was born in 1980, and her second daughter was born five years later in 1985. Patricia and her husband purchased their first home in 1985. At that point, motivated by life circumstances, she began a journey of personal growth and achievement. She first obtained her real estate license and worked as a successful realtor for several years. This was followed by several jobs that involved working on a personal level with individuals. She later received a certificate, state license, associate degree, and finally, a bachelor's degree. This allowed her to work professionally in the field of human services and addiction counseling. Based on a recommendation of a close friend who had contributed to the Overcoming Mediocrity book series, she became very interested in also telling her story. Patricia wanted to share with other women, her children, and grandchildren the importance of raising awareness regarding addiction. This project is important on many different levels. It allows her to share the devasting and sabotaging impact that substance abuse can have on many lives. It affects not only the person using it but also all others involved. This allows her to plant a seed for those who may be struggling with substance abuse themselves or their loved ones.

Patricia Marie Larsen
1022 West Gramercy Lane
Addison, IL 60101
630-542-4315
PatriciaLarsen@comcast.net

# Faly Colaizzi

## *Discovering My Superpower*

The sky split open with a bolt of lightning. A storm was coming. As nightfall slammed hard that evening, my father cast his shadow. I stood frozen in the front foyer of our house. My eyes were fixated on an oil painting of my mother. She was a beauty queen in her native country of Spain. In the portrait, her eyes shone with confidence, and her olive-soft skin glowed. No one would doubt for a moment that the world lay at her feet.

I glanced toward the dining room and saw her struggle, as my father brutally pulled her into the kitchen. My heart pounded. My face slumped as if it were about to wipe the floor. He held her so tight that I could hear her choking on her nightgown collar. At that moment, I mentally left my body. I was only four years old. All I wanted to do was save her. My soul cried at the injustice.

I heard him slam her against the wall. I heard the doorframe crack and the sound of twisted wood screeching to its breaking point. I caught his barking screams in my bones as our home's foundation shook.

*"I'M GOING TO TEAR YOU APART!"*

Deafening slaps and pummeling cracks rippled in my core. She cried, then whimpered. *"NO, HENRIK... No!"* I could have filled my ears with cement and still heard the desperation in her voice.

I crept toward the kitchen. She huddled in the corner, her skin torn, bloodied bruises forming on her arms. As she took blow after blow, she fell silent. His python-like arm was wrapped around her neck, pulling her back as she grabbed for the twisted door frame. Reaching his boiling point, his voice split the night… I couldn't make out the tirade, yet the vibration shook the windows.

I stood in the doorway for what seemed to be an eternity. I saw my mom's contusions and her shredded nightgown. Shaking, I locked eyes with my father. My little girl mind already knew that he was a pathological terrorist and needed to be stopped. However, I didn't have the language for it. I already understood that he was searching for an out to his purposeless life.

My mother eventually tried to leave him and raise my sister and me alone. However, he continued to torture us. As the painful decades melted away, my mom, sister, and I choked on my father's bitter poison.

Navigating abuse is never easy. However, it can sometimes take an awakening to understand that it is indeed happening to you. This is especially true when discord is all you've known since birth. In my destructive and toxic relationship with my father, I witnessed a lifetime of abuse against my mother. My father's manipulation and control were woven into our lives like snake venom. While my mother stood strong and unsinkable against my father's relentless wrath, little did I know that I would become his next victim.

I was in my mid-thirties when I found myself in the waiting room of my psychotherapist's office. As I sat there, I had a flashback. My mom, sister, and I were hiding at our local grocery store when we saw our father's car swing slowly by. We instinctively moved down an aisle and hid behind the soup cans, as my mom watched his car turn the corner. He was trying to hunt us down.

I had hundreds of memories like this one. I had been in therapy for years. Some days were good, and some days were not so good. At times, everything in my brain seemed to bother me and get in my way. Everything felt messy. It was like I was shoveling through piles of mental scar tissue. There were days that I didn't want to do the work. I was feeling pity for myself. Why was I in therapy, when my father needed to be locked up in a hospital for all the madness that he unleashed?

I was not only angry with what my father put my mother through. I was also angry with what he put my sister and me through, with all I had experienced through my father's explosive tirades, mind control, and tyrannical bullying. I knew this animal had irreversibly destroyed that part of my life. The tidal wave from the past was crashing down around me. I would get up from one wave, and another would bear down. I could hear him in my sleep, with the barking orders and verbal assaults. I wore the abuse like a tattoo. The memories from my childhood came at me like a freight train. What surfaced was consuming grief.

My only freedom was in my isolation inside a hell I couldn't escape. These were all symptoms of hopelessness fueled by anxiety and depression in my search for meaning and a new foundation. With my father, I had no voice. I was always inside a world of abuse, anger, and rage. Many scars had forged a concrete barrier to a healthy and happy future. I didn't even know what that kind of future could look like.

The truth was that I wanted to destroy him. He had no right to be happy after destroying us. Over the years, I had lived with the stress of his unstable behaviors. I was piggybacking off of his rage.

For me, this feeling wasn't right. It wasn't who I was in my soul. However, I wanted justice for my mother. I wanted to make right all that was wrong. However, I couldn't. I wanted revenge. I wanted the childhood that was taken from me. Instead of sitting in a doctor's office trying to figure out the emptiness I felt inside, I wanted my peace. I lived wedged between a world of coping skills and avoidance and the urge to fight back. I tried many strategies to thwart my grandiose, malignant, sociopathic, narcissistic father… but nothing worked.

The turning point came on the afternoon when my mother stood in court awaiting her divorce after nine years of marriage and a five-year battle. My father had taken 90% of their estate and had left us with a $14,000 lien against our home. The clock was ticking with the threat of a forced sale. My mother already had no alimony and barely enough money for food and bills. However, my mother desperately wanted out and had no choice but to sign all legal documents or face contempt of court and jail time.

My father had paid off judges, lawyers, and police officers, to negotiate an annulment. He also boasted that my sister and I were illegitimate bastard children. Hearing the judge's final ruling, my mother's knees buckled, and she collapsed in the courtroom.

That could have been the end of a sad story. However, nothing could break my mother. I had lived through every moment with her and had endured her pain as if it were happening to me. I had my mother's spirit, and I was never going to follow down the path of the broken. At that moment, **I vowed justice, somehow, someway!**

Years passed. I had now endured over forty-five years of my father's terrorist reign. I knew things had to change, so I took matters into my own hands. I moved into the core of my spirit and found myself standing in the living room of my father's home. He began talking to me about the half-acre of land that was adjacent to his house. He had put the land in my name and was worried that my sister's soon-to-be ex-husband would try and get his hands on it. Out of nowhere, my father started to scream at me. *"YOUR SISTER IS JUST GOING TO GIVE THIS LAND AWAY... GOD DAMN IT!"* Spit flew from his mouth.

As I stood in his living room that day, something came over me. Sparks seemed to lift me from my feet. I felt as if I was flying as I met him in the dining room where he stood.

I found dark octaves I never knew I had. *"YOU'RE JUST A GOD DAMN BULLY!"* my voice thundered, finally drowning out my father's cruel, belligerent tone.

My voice was louder, stronger, and more vicious for the first time. Years of abuse and scorn poured out of my soul. Fire raged from my mouth. *"SHUT UP... SHUT UP! How dare you continuously scold me! SHUT THE HELL UP!"*

My father's jaw dropped. His face fell, dumbfounded at the animosity in my voice. He fell to the couch. Dizzy, I walked outside, my blood pressure pulsing, my breath rough... yet I never felt more alive. I had done it... I had shut down the bully!

I was old enough to have a bird's eye view of my life and had developed the ability to reflect on the atrocities that I witnessed. I had also gotten clear in my mind and body that I was being physically and mentally abused. What moved me through the injustice was time, soul-searching therapies, and cutting the umbilical cord on toxic people. History doesn't care about your baggage. However, your future does.

I ultimately chose to move forward with my life and away from the chaos. On my journey, I discovered that I had a superpower that would help me find my voice. I **became an author!** I empowered myself in a way where I could be heard and where no one could take that away from me. This was a new world that I could create, a new space where I could expose the truth and wrongdoings and make things right again.

I worked on my own psychological profile of my father. I dissected every last disturbing behavior putting together a summary of who he was. I categorized every narcissistic and sociopathic predisposition, by carefully creating a map of his unhinged madness.

In my most recent novel, *Unsinkable Princess*, I created a behavioral checklist identifying the behaviors of a sociopathic narcissist. If you find yourself awake at night being terrorized by a family member, a boss, or a significant other, make yourself comfortable with this checklist. If you can identify more than one behavior, you have a few choices to make. You can try and defuse the narcissist, you can stay in the abuse, or you can choose to leave the situation completely. If you decide to stay, understand that the narcissist will never have you in their best interest. Their world only centers around themselves. Try to move into action. Don't stay in the abuse. Don't waste the time that I did. Recognize the abusive relationship and plan to break free.

Staying only allows the perpetrator to think that how they treat you is okay. Do not fear retaliation. This is your life.

*Unsinkable Princess* is the unprecedented story of abuse and a cruel divorce that has never been documented before, where a minefield of chaos, scandal, attempted murder, domestic abuse, mental and emotional torture, criminal behavior, corruption, betrayal, pathological narcissism, and an unparalleled obstruction of justice, threaten to destroy the lives of a mother and her two daughters. It is a story of how our mother became our hero and how I found my empowerment. This is a guidebook to transcendence that will take you from where you are to where you want to be.

I love being a voice for the ones who hide in the shadows of abuse and helping them find the light to expose the truth. In giving back, my philanthropy work centers around women and children who don't have enough. Things will always come full circle when you can give back to others who may be going through their own traumas. Transformation away from tragedy is one of the greatest gifts you can give yourself, as you shed the skin of the past and live in the grace surrounding you.

**Faly Colaizzi**

Faly Colaizzi was born and raised in the Chicagoland area. She graduated from Illinois State University with a Bachelor of Science degree. She has a 33-year career as a Business Development Manager and enjoys being a strong voice for her clients. She is a member of the Board of Education Committee for BOMA Chicago, a member of the Western Loss Association, and she was the first female president of the Blue Goose Association in her industry. She is the mom of two thriving boys and is committed to her philanthropy work through the Saint Charles Women's Club. She has also served on the Saint Charles Women's Club board for two consecutive years. She has many favorite charities serving women, children, animal shelters, and local food banks. She is also an ambassador and guest speaker for the Eversight Eye Bank.

Faly Colaizzi is the author of two fiction novels in the Haunted Nights at Drumheller Castle series. Faly is proud to be part of this amazing group of ladies and book series, Overcoming Mediocrity. As Faly delves into her own personal struggles in her latest autobiographical and biographical novel *Unsinkable Princess* (out late 2023), you will discover yourself down the rabbit hole in a world of unparalleled scandal, betrayal, and deceit. Faly hopes to shed light on domestic violence and tyrannical narcissism. This is with her unique story of her mother's incredible life and the bully that tried to shut her down. If Faly can help even one soul salvage their life back, she has done her job.

Faly Colaizzi
Faly Colaizzi on Facebook, LinkedIn
Falita@comcast.net
www.drumhellercastle.com

# Kim Falco

## *My Bucket*

It had been almost a year since my divorce. I survived an abusive nine-year marriage, and I was broken. I felt like I was in a dream disconnected as I watched my daughters playing, almost as if I was flying above my life, wondering how I ended up here. It was two weeks since my surgery, and I was still bleeding, unable to regain my strength, and spending most of my day lying on the couch. Crippled with fear and exhaustion, I worried that I would not be able to play at the park, take them to school, or manage basic "momming." (Tapping into the reserves of strength you never knew you had, juggling all the things, getting by on less sleep than you ever thought possible, etc.) I was a single mother with four small girls at 29 years old. I was terrified, and depression was a daily battle. I was losing hope. My hair was falling out, and it became an obsession. I would count the hairs in the drain because I read it was normal to lose 100 hairs a day… which stressed me out and made more hair fall out.

As I lay there, I caught my oldest daughter looking at me, tears welling up in her eyes. I could see that she was worried. She knew I wasn't myself. I was sick and not getting better. She was caring for her sisters and helping me with chores. She had to grow up very fast. It broke my heart to see her so scared and to know what she was going through and if she was wondering if this was our "new normal."

How did superstar Kim end up here? I was a disciplined athlete, captain of my gymnastics team, top of my class, and a Beauty Queen. Now, I was alone, sick, and going bald. This is not how I imagined my life.

I knew I had to regain my strength, or I would lose everything. *It was time to get up and fight.* I started to think about my holistic lifestyle and how traditional medical treatment was not working. I began my search for a holistic doctor who I believed could help me.

This is where my journey back started. Not only did I need to regain my strength and my health, but I needed to find my ability to be hopeful again.

**Hope for New Beginnings**

I started thinking about my past experiences, accomplishments, and the mindset and skills required to set goals and succeed in those situations. I realized that not only did I have the tools, but I could apply them to this challenge I was facing. *I was not a quitter; I was a winner.*

After many hours of research, I finally found a holistic doctor. He was well-known and respected, so I eagerly made the appointment. I knew this was the first step in my healing process, and it would take a lot of work and discipline to get to where I wanted to be. The doctor was very compassionate as I told my story. He could see that it was more than the physical symptoms I was struggling with. There were emotional issues as well. He asked me if I believed in God, which startled me at first, but it was like a light switch. I had been so overwhelmed after my divorce and trying to raise four little girls that I lost sight of my faith when I needed God the most. I couldn't see him through the fog. He put his hand on mine and asked if he could pray with me. I started to weep. I knew God was there with me, and things would be all right. The doctor recommended supplements, a special diet, prayer, and visualization. It was all about being disciplined, much like when I was a gymnast or studying for a big test.

Early morning juicing, walks with the kids, and visualizing that my body was healing, I saw the light going through my body, healing it inch by inch. I prayed on my knees to God every day, and I knew he was listening. During that time, although being a single mom was not easy by any means, I tried not to let negative thoughts consume me, even when money was tight and I worried about paying the bills. I would pray and tell God I was grateful for being alive and for my beautiful little girls. One morning I went to get the mail, and inside I found an envelope, there was no writing on it, just an envelope. I opened it, and there was $400 in cash. I was overwhelmed and praised God for his miracles. To this day, I do not know how it got there.

Several months later, I was healed in more ways than one. I was back to work and running around with my girls. Not long after that, I met a wonderful man. He was very kind, and having someone in my life who treated me with love and respect was refreshing. A year later, we were married and running a busy blended family and two businesses. With my four daughters and his three kids, we were a modern-day "Brady Bunch."

**Kim Was Winning Again**

Looking back, I realize that my experiences, accomplishments, skills, network of people, and faith had given me the strength to take the next steps and the next leap. It was my "bucket" of tools I had acquired since I was a young girl. It was everything I learned; everyone I knew. I started thinking about how I had it all stored in my head. I would then unpack my bucket and write down what I had stored there by category. I realized that I was filling my "bucket" daily and started to be more conscious of my experiences, what I learned that day, who I met, and what challenges I overcame. I started journaling to track what I was learning and created a resource list by category: Experiences, Skills, Network/Relationships, and Faith. I still get excited when I learn something new and say, *"Wow! That is going in my bucket."*

Everyone has their own "bucket" filled with experiences, skills, and networks. When you sort them all out in categories, you can see how they can transfer into a new career, take on a challenge you are facing, or a new life path. I have used my "bucket" many times in my life. For instance, I was making a life-changing move to Southwest Florida. I knew I had to be fearless and trust God and my abilities to embark on this new adventure. My many experiences with life changes helped me to have the confidence to just leap.

I needed to refer to my "bucket" again when I saw that a Chamber Executive position opened with the Bonita Springs Chamber of Commerce. Still, it required a college degree and/or certification in organizational management. Unfortunately, I did not have either. Despite that, I knew I was qualified, so I applied for the position. I created an "Experiential Resume" promoting the experience and skills I learned while working as a realtor and my background in marketing, which would transfer into this position. I was offered the position and jumped in full speed ahead. Working for the Chamber of Commerce was very challenging, and I felt that I was learning so much and building my worth daily. During that time, I met many different people from the business community as well as respected leaders in government and organizations area-wide. Your network is a very important part of your "bucket." It is your resource for referrals, new opportunities, and support.

To this day, I use my "bucket" to take on anything that comes my way, including challenges and opportunities. I think back to that day, sitting on the couch. I wonder what our lives would have been like if I had given up. I am grateful every day that I got up and fought; it has been quite the journey ever since. Life is full of beautiful moments and also filled with hard times and tough challenges. Knowing you have the resources from all you have learned will help you overcome the hard times and give you the confidence to move upward and onward.

Remember to fill your "bucket" every day with all you learn and who you meet along the way.

Create a journal and organize it by categories. You will see how amazing you are. These days, I am so blessed to have four beautiful daughters who have grown into strong, confident women. I am enjoying spending time with my six grandchildren and look forward to watching them grow up. Thank God he reached out to me that day in the doctor's office. It was the turning point in my life that saved me.

God bless you all.

# Kim Falco

Kim Falco is the consummate personable, engaging, self-assured professional; she is an extraordinarily effective networker who forms friendly relationships readily and is a top-notch sales professional.

Because of her diverse experience and background, Kim brings a savvy marketing sense to everything she touches. She is an aggressive matchmaker who leverages her contacts to build her brand and promote the success of everyone she meets.

Kim currently serves as National Director of Sales and is highly regarded in her field. She is entrenched in industry associations, organizations, and her community and recently served as an elected official in her county. She has been invited to speak at industry events and conferences where she brings her light-hearted touch and humor to the world of governmental finance.

She developed her winning sales and negotiating skills while she was a member of her family's top-producing, award-winning Real Estate Team, which was recognized nationwide. Kim was focused on a consultative approach to sales, fine-tuning her craft by providing support and educating her clients throughout the process.

Kim took on a new challenge working for a five-star accredited Chamber of Commerce, utilizing her knowledge of sales and marketing to increase revenues by introducing new opportunities for sponsorship and investment into the organization. She used her networking skills to connect and build strong business alliances throughout the organization and community.

Kim credits her success to the people she has met along the way; friendships, mentors, and colleagues, all having some nugget to share or lesson to teach, filling her bucket. But her most rewarding role is as a proud mother and grandmother.

Kim enjoys the outdoors, whether it be walking on the beach or hiking in the woods. You can find her these days riding around on her motorcycle through the streets of the quaint lake town she calls home.

Kim Falco
Wisconsin
kfalco@acspro.us

# Elizabeth Rose Daily-Izquierdo

## *Are You Waiting for a Crisis?*

*"She stood in the storm, and when the wind did not blow her away, she adjusted her sails."*

—Elizabeth Edwards

### When the Storm Rolled In

The storm began in December of 2009. My life was thrown into a storm of hardships that would put every ounce of my fortitude, faith, and strength to the test. As beautiful snowflakes delicately fell from the skies to cover the earth in a tranquil white, the initial gusts of turmoil arrived unannounced. My husband had recently undergone a quadruple bypass following his third heart attack when he inexplicably suffered his fourth heart attack a few months later. This was all a sobering reminder of life's frailty as if nature itself was trying to make me aware of how fragile our existence was.

### As the Calendar Pages Turned to February, Another Storm Cloud Rolled In.

My husband of 25 years, my companion who had walked beside me through the victorious highs and heartbreaking valleys of life, made the decision that he wanted to start over and embarked on a new path. This decision was based on a combination of life pressures, midlife introspection, decades of marital complexities, and the mounting burdens of health struggles. His departure left behind an echoing silence, a void that seemed to foretell even greater challenges looming on the horizon.

## The Grief

The first deluge of distress arrived with the heart-wrenching loss of Woody, our loyal and cherished Bird Dog Lab, whose life was claimed by the relentless grasp of bone cancer, marking the beginning of the grief. The agonizing decision to release our faithful friend from his pain was a mere prelude to the heartbreak that would soon descend upon us. Woody was our companion, our protector, and our greatest buddy.

After Woody passed, I made the decision to visit the doctor and get a checkup. After years of putting off taking care of myself, I realized how important it was to do so. After all, I have not had one in more than ten years. *I am happy I went*. They discovered that the multiple lesions on my thyroid were cancerous. Fortunately, my doctor quickly identified them. The gift of early discovery showed the way forward, even in the face of this frightening truth. She gave me back my life. She saved my life, and I am eternally grateful for it.

After that, lightning struck. One of my family members passed away every four months for the next 1.5 years. My Aunt in Ireland left first, followed by my dad, my Aunt Jenny, my Uncle Jack, and lastly, my mom (all of whom left in four-month intervals). Even the funeral director found it hard to believe. *It was a grim time.* We have not experienced death in that way in an exceptionally long time.

> *"We love them.*
> *We miss them.*
> *We grieve them.*
> *And so, we live our lives,*
> *to make them proud."*

## Financial Storm

Things got a lot worse as the financial storm raged alongside the personal and emotional turmoil. With only one source of income, the bills were piling up, and my home teetered on the brink of forbearance — not just once, but twice. I took out five or six payday loans a month to cover the mortgage because I had to protect my family's home. I came within a few hours of losing my house several times. I can still vividly remember the intense fear I had as I hurried from one Payday Loan establishment to another in an effort to have enough money to pay the mortgage and the previous month's bills. The only thing I knew was that if I could not get the money to the bank in time, *I would lose my home.*

At the time, there were no limitations on the number of debts a person may have. At any given time, I could take out as many loans as I could find in places that would give them to me. Since then, state laws have changed. Once I had enough cash on hand to pay the debt, I needed to arrive at a Western Union in plenty of time to send the money. The banks had a cutoff time of 3 p.m. CST. I am not sure how I got by in a few situations. It was through God's mercy and my own willpower that it was still possible to try. Regardless of how ridiculous that sounded, *I never gave up and continued.*

**And If That Was Not Enough…**

Later, I was involved in a car accident that damaged my vehicle, leaving me unable to get to work or pay my obligations. There were times when *I felt completely alone,* but the more I thought about it, the more I understood that was not the case.

**There Are Rainbows Even During Storms.**

Moments of generosity and hope made me realize *I was not alone.* My coworkers generously donated their work hours to me so that I could earn more money. When I did not have a vehicle to get to work, Dilyss and Sandra graciously loaned me their cars so I would not lose my jobs. Karen never gave up on me and kept trying to stay in touch until I finally answered. The neighborhood food bank also provided support for my family, and of course, God was there to guide me through this.

**I Refer to this Season… As A Storm… For These Reasons…**

I persisted throughout, learning that *it was never too late until it was too late.* **Never Give Up!** Defying doubt and skepticism, I embarked on a journey to return to school to finish my bachelor's degree. It was crucial for me to graduate and get my degree. I was juggling multiple jobs at the time, attending evening classes, and surviving on mere fragments of sleep. The norm was ten cups of coffee each day to keep up with my robotic routine. If I had an unplanned day off, my body did not know how to slow down or take a break. I had a strong sense of direction and was determined to reach my goals. I was determined to get my degree!

**Never Doubt Yourself**

There were many skeptics, including relatives and coworkers, who would say, *"Oh... What are you doing?" "You are getting too old." "That is too expensive. Absolutely pointless."* It was hard to keep from doubting myself. It was difficult to overcome the negative inner critics who constantly told me I was not good enough. The only reason I had faith in my ability to succeed was that **I Never Gave Up** and understood that there was still time.

*"Don't ever doubt yourself.*
*You can do anything you put your mind to.*
*All you have to do is believe in YOU."*

—Jenny Charbonneau

At age 59, I reached a milestone that symbolized more than academic success; it showed my strength and determination. I was the first person in my immediate family to graduate from college and earn a bachelor's degree.

**The Storm Passed**

I make a point of *never taking anything for granted*. That we possess the strength to rewrite our narrative. Hopefully, I have gained wisdom from my mistakes. Life is rarely a straight line, and it frequently takes a different route than what you had intended. Although it occasionally feels like a roller coaster or can be bumpy, it is never too late to give it your all.

Challenges will test us, push us to our limits, and challenge our endurance.

Within the midst of these challenges, we uncover our inner fortitude, our capacity to persevere, and the unwavering spirit that defines us.

For those who find themselves navigating their own storms, remember that after the rain, the sky clears, the sun shines once more, and rainbows rise.

Amidst the chaos, there is always room for hope, growth, and the triumphant overcoming of adversity.

Through it all, our spirit remains unbroken, resilient, and ever-hopeful, ready to face the challenges of life's journey.

# Elizabeth Rose Daily-Izquierdo

Elizabeth Izquierdo is a mother of two amazing young men, a grandmother with two beautiful grandsons, a successful administrative professional at a $100B global logistics company, and an advocate for the position that it is never too late to… chase your dreams, achieve your goals and fulfill your passions! Elizabeth has a bachelor's degree in international business and a Master's Certificate in The Essentials of Business Acumen. She is Microsoft Power BI certified and is currently working towards a master's degree.

Along the way, Elizabeth never missed an opportunity to encourage other women to seek out their purpose and fulfill their ambitions, championing education as the key to unlocking doors and breaking chains. Elizabeth unfailingly shared resources and encouraged others in their journeys.

She began working toward her educational goal over 40 years ago, and at the age of 59, she was the first among her immediate family to earn a college degree. This journey was anything but a straight line. Along the way, Elizabeth raised a family, has maintained full-time employment for 33+ years, and has simultaneously part-time employment for 22+ years. She is a lifelong learner, loves to read, enjoys gardening, and craves eating green vegetables of any kind.

Elizabeth has felt a calling to teach others that you are never too old, it is never too late to start a goal, and that grace, mercy, grit, and resilience will all bring you over the finish line. She wants to demonstrate that everyone has the power within them to succeed and live their best life. This opportunity provides the medium to express these teachings.

Elizabeth Rose Daily-Izquierdo
ERIzquierdo@gmail.com

# Ruby Williams

## *Embracing A Life Beyond Alcohol*

**Groundhog's Day**

It's 4:55 p.m., and I'm finally done with work. The day has been a whirlwind of decisions and putting out fires at my corporate job in the wine industry. I told myself this morning that today would be different, that I wouldn't drink again. I even got rid of all the alcohol in the house to prove my determination. But as the day wore on, thoughts of wine began to consume me.

I walk towards my car, repeating in my mind that I'll head straight home and resist the temptation to buy wine. But I can't resist the allure of the tasting room, the tourists enjoying themselves, and the beautiful vineyards. Before I know it, I'm already there. My inner voice screams at me not to buy it, so I grab a mini bottle of champagne for the ride home. I need that immediate relief because my brain feels possessed. I try to rationalize, telling myself it's just a mini bottle and I won't have enough to cause any problems.

Yet, the self-loathing intensifies as I berate myself for not being able to stick to my promise. I finish the mini bottle and stop at the grocery store for another two bottles, as one is never enough. I ignore the voice telling me not to go inside. I feel ashamed and worthless, believing that buying this wine must mean I really do have a problem. But at the same time, there's a strange sense of relief, as if everything will be okay tonight. I'll try to stop again tomorrow, I tell myself.

Once home, I pour one glass while cooking dinner, and then a second while eating and watching T.V. I don't realize it, but I'm on autopilot and drink until I pass out on the couch. In the early hours of the morning, I wake up, seeing two empty bottles on the coffee table, not even remembering drinking the second one at all.

I look at myself in the mirror, and I don't recognize the person staring back at me — a liar, a horrible person with bloodshot eyes. In desperation, I hide the bottles at the bottom of the recycling bin, not wanting to face them tomorrow. I get to bed but spend hours tossing and turning, heart racing, full of despair, and in utter anguish as I beg for help. I worry about my health, liver, and heart and promise myself that I won't drink again tomorrow. But the cycle repeats itself like Groundhog's Day. I wake up feeling exhausted, dehydrated, brain fog, and sick to my stomach. Despite knowing how much worse things are becoming, I try to convince myself that I can manage it.

But deep down, I know I'm losing control. Nevertheless, I try to be hopeful, telling myself that today will be different. However, the same patterns emerge, and I find myself stuck in this vicious loop, feeling trapped and desperate for a way out. I feel like the wine glass can never be big enough. I feel chained to it and increasingly isolated, as my life gets smaller and smaller...

**You Are Not Alone, and It's Not Your Fault**

I felt so alone and that this was only happening to me. I asked myself, *"Why don't I have the willpower to stop drinking? What's wrong with me? Why am I so weak in this area but strong in other areas of my life?"*

Looking back, it all started with food addiction, as I had weight issues growing up and numbed my emotions with food. After a home foreclosure, a child custody battle with my ex-husband, and the stress of being a single mom with a demanding job, I gained over one hundred pounds in a brief time. My solution was to have weight loss surgery. Cutting out part of my stomach worked, as I lost all the extra weight, but because I didn't address my thoughts, feelings, beliefs, and reasons why I wanted to numb, I transferred my binge eating to alcohol addiction. Before the surgery, I was on a slower trajectory to becoming addicted to alcohol, so this fast-moving change caught me completely off guard.

What is addiction? It's nothing more than an up-and-down cycle. You consume something (sugar, drugs, alcohol... it doesn't matter), and you feel better temporarily, so you consume the same substance again. But this time, it doesn't feel quite as good as your subconscious mind remembers, so you need a little bit more. Then the effects wear off, and you consume it again. It's a high-and-low cycle that keeps you coming back to whatever substance you subconsciously believe makes you feel better. ***Addiction can happen to anyone, and it's not your fault!***

So, let me ask you...

- Are you living life to your full potential?
- Could alcohol be that one big domino keeping you stuck in mediocrity?
- How much of your time, energy, and vitality have you wasted on alcohol?
- What's possible if you eliminate just one thing, alcohol?

## Why Does Alcohol Get a Free Pass in Our Society?

Let's face it: alcohol is EVERYWHERE!

- Come out for a girls' night at the bar. Let's go wine tasting for the bachelorette party.
- Wine with dinner is necessary on date night. It's your birthday, and we always celebrate with champagne.
- You must meet the clients for happy hour or a drink on the golf course to make the sales deal. And margaritas after work.
- Drink to survive the pandemic and motherhood. Let's plan a "playdate" for the kids, and we'll drink vodka (LOL).
- Just drink alcohol to have fun, fit in, and go to family gatherings, events, concerts, weddings, vacations, school functions, restaurants, parties, funerals, and baby showers — drink to do everything!
- Alcohol is in ads, commercials, T.V. shows, movies, and social media — it's everywhere!
- My family and friends drink, my coworkers and boss drink — everyone drinks!
- Oh! Don't forget mimosas at brunch, beer at ball games, and wine at the book club.

The message is that you need alcohol to have fun and require it at every celebration. Then, you begin to need it to get through each weekday. The truth is alcohol causes cancer, depression, anxiety, stress, disrupts sleep, and increases memory loss, fat storage, and premature aging. The list of negative effects is quite extensive.

Together, let's unravel the veil of alcohol in our lives to be present and authentic, discover ourselves, and become liberated from the shackles of a culture that no longer serves our highest good. There is a world of possibility where genuine connections and true joy await us, untainted by the influence of the alcohol industry.

**Fresh Solutions and Hope**

A new path emerged after losing my wine industry job. My cousin suggested I read "This Naked Mind" by Annie Grace. I took radical responsibility for my drinking and did the work to free myself from alcohol. I now help individuals who want to change their relationship with alcohol. By using a coaching methodology alternative to Alcoholics Anonymous (A.A.), I can guide you through this process to change your alcohol habit. You don't need to stop drinking right away in my program.

- It all starts with awareness, grace, and curiosity, without judgment.
- Initially, you'll acquire new knowledge, then adjust your perspectives, reframe your beliefs, connect with your emotions, and finally, change your behavior.
- You choose when to take a break from alcohol.
- Address the reasons why you drink and practice self-compassion.
- I have the tools, tactics, and coaching expertise to guide you.
- Are you open to learning how to finally control alcohol?

By removing alcohol, you will gain trust in yourself again and feel healthy. I lost weight and have so much energy. I set goals and accomplish them. I am a better friend and mother. I sleep soundly, and my productivity is off the charts. My brain healed, and I finally figured out how to practice meditation. I feel calm, grateful, and have clarity again. I am living a life with a future full of possibilities!

Imagine it's 6 a.m., and you wake up effortlessly and well-rested. The house is quiet, and do you…

- Get yourself a cup of coffee and sit down with your journal. You love reflecting in the morning.
- You meditate and say your prayers or affirmations; morning is your spiritual time.

- Get your yoga pants on to practice salutations and exercise with the sunrise.
- Take your dog for a walk and enjoy nature because you own your mornings.

In a heartbeat, you'll realize you no longer want this life with alcohol. Choose to reclaim yourself and embrace the path to true freedom. Like me, you can regain your power and begin to feel better.

*This is your only life.*

*Make it epic!*


P.S. My grandpa just celebrated his 104th birthday, and I am half his age. I had the realization that I "get" to live another whole lifetime. I get to live this "second" lifetime alcohol-free and healthy. There is so much HOPE!

# Ruby Williams

In the heart of Ruby Williams' transformative journey lies an inspiring tale of liberation and empowerment. Breaking free from the clutches of alcohol in May 2019, Ruby's triumph ignited a cascade of positive changes — shedding pounds, reclaiming vitality, and achieving long-held dreams. Today, Ruby Williams stands tall as a beacon of hope and an Alcohol Freedom Coach, driven by a resolute mission: to guide those who want to change their relationship with alcohol and move to a path of profound transformation.

With the potent tools of the This Naked Mind coaching methodology at her disposal, Ruby masterfully wields the art of questioning during her sessions. These dynamic exchanges have the potential to catalyze shifts in mindset, leading to a balance where alcohol assumes a marginal role. By unshackling individuals from the grip of alcohol, Ruby empowers them to embrace possibilities, discovering passions they might never have otherwise explored.

With nearly two decades as a wine industry professional, Ruby's past is marked by a relentless cycle of daily drinking as a coping tool for stress. Wrestling with drinking more than intended, she found herself ensnared in a struggle that defied self-rescue, exacerbated by the inseparable ties between her identity and the wine culture. Drawing from her personal journey, Ruby specializes in guiding women who've grappled with alcohol-induced weight gain following bariatric surgery. Armed with empathy born from her own experiences, she guides transformation.

Ruby's dedication extends to crafting lives enriched with fulfillment, vitality, and harmony — liberated from alcohol's stranglehold. Residing just an hour north of San Francisco, she is the proud mother of an adult son, and along with her dog and chickens, she finds gratitude in daily meditation and yoga practice.

Ruby Williams
Freedom Renegade Coaching
Sebastopol, CA 95472
Ruby.Williams@FreedomRenegadeCoaching.com
www.FreedomRenegadeCoaching.com

## 4 Simple Steps: Experience A Wine-Free Weekend

Why not take a leap of faith with me? Embrace a WINE-FREE WEEKEND with "4 Simple Steps."

Alcohol Freedom Coach Ruby Williams created the perfect guide for you, which includes:

- ♥ A comprehensive worksheet to get you super prepared for the weekend.
- ♥ An inspiring video to ignite your motivation.
- ♥ Proven strategies to conquer cravings.
- ♥ Tools for navigating the weekend effortlessly.
- ♥ A follow-up assessment to gauge your progress.

You can enjoy social gatherings without wine. Discover the possibilities!

Grab your FREE guide and get started this Friday!

https://coachingwithruby.com/EpicWomen

Each episode features today's top influencers and entrepreneurs on the rise as they share empowering stories and ninja tips meant to become the

## FUEL TO IGNITE
a positive change in your life.

bit.ly/mupodcr

# YOUR STORY

## Harness the Power of Story
to Build Your Brand & Attract Clients.

# FREE GIFT

Learn how your story can position you uniquely in the marketplace, attract clients, and distinguish yourself from all competition.

OvercomingMediocrity.org/Freebie

www.ingramcontent.com/pod-product-compliance
Lightning Source LLC
Chambersburg PA
CBHW061312110426
42742CB00012BA/2162